POSSIBILITY IS YOUR SUPER POWER

VICTORIA ALONSO

WITH CECILIA MOLINARI

POSSIBILITY IS YOUR SUPER POWER

UNLOCK YOUR ENDLESS POTENTIAL

HYPERION AVENUE

LOS ANGELES   NEW YORK

First Edition, September 2025
1 3 5 7 9 10 8 6 4 2
FAC-004510-25170
Printed in the United States of America

This book is set in Gotham, DIN, and Chronicle Text
Designed by Amy C. King

Library of Congress Control Number: 2025934918
ISBN 978-1-368-09008-7

Reinforced binding
www.HyperionAvenueBooks.com

To my kid, Raven, the kindest, most thoughtful
and funny human I know. You are the greatest gift
and the brightest light in my life. The strength
of your voice and the power of possibility will
always be within you. Don't let anyone define
you but yourself. I will be by your side to
watch you shine for the next fifty summers!

Contents

Introduction

Acknowledgments

Introduction

"All I need is possible."

—DR. STRANGE, *DOCTOR STRANGE* (2016)

As is the case in all superhero and human origin stories, I had no clue what the future would hold for me when I came into this world. I never thought I'd work in the film industry; I never thought I'd produce superhero movies; I never thought I'd write a book. I was just one of the hundreds of thousands of kids in Argentina who were growing up amid a heart-wrenching military dictatorship, trying to figure out this thing called life. Yet my mother instilled in me from a young age the belief that anything was possible if I set my mind to it. As I grew older, I learned how to follow my gut, consider my options, and lead with a yes instead of a no when presented with new and intriguing choices along my path. Eventually, this mindset inspired me to leave my hometown of La Plata at fifteen and say yes to studying abroad in the United States. Never in my wildest dreams did I imagine that this one decision would eventually open the door to so many unique and remarkable opportunities.

Once I began to define my path as a storyteller and a decision maker, I sought out every door possible to enter the film industry: the side doors, the back doors, the doggy doors. And I jumped at the first opportunity I received to become a production assistant—a yes that, without knowing the first thing about film production at the time, kick-started a long and prosperous career. By taking that leap, I managed to work my way up the proverbial ladder that led me to visual effects production jobs at Sony, Paramount, Fox, and DreamWorks. I hit exciting milestones throughout this long and winding road of filmmaking, which ultimately catalyzed me into becoming the president of physical and postproduction, visual effects, and animation production of Marvel Studios, home to the Marvel Cinematic Universe, the highest-grossing film franchise of all time.

Devoting eighteen years of my career to bringing relatable superheroes to the big screen has paved the way for me to share with you one simple secret: You don't need a cape, a shield, or the power of flight to be your own superhero. If you are willing to quiet the outside chatter and listen to yourself, to what you want and need, you will realize that the answers are already there, waiting to be discovered within you.

I'm not here to give you a one-size-fits-all magic formula to success, because I'm keenly aware that each of our paths is beautifully and uniquely different. What I do hope to do is to inspire and empower you to tap into your full potential, listen to your voice, and open yourself up to your ultimate superpower: *possibility*. My strength, resilience, and perseverance are major contributors along my road to success, but I believe considering and saying yes to possibilities is the fuel that has bolstered my journey to exhilarating new heights.

In *Possibility Is Your Superpower*, there are no right or wrong ways to apply possibility to your life, because each person's potential is different and in tune with their own path. So I won't be asking you to meditate or do exercises or journal. All I would like is for you to simply take the time to consider the possibilities presented in this book so that you too may be inspired to take an active role in your fate. How old you are doesn't matter, nor does your religion, your race, your ethnicity, your sexual preferences, what you have or don't have, or where in life you may be. Every road, every path, every journey, every life begins with possibility. Oftentimes all it takes is opening that one door in front of you to discover a new realm of opportunities. When in doubt, remember this: At the end of the day, you are just as strong as the superheroes you've been looking up to since you were a kid, because their power and your own ultimately spring from character, will, resolve, and the ability to embrace the possibilities along your path.

My hope is that by sharing a deep dive into my life and career—the hurdles, the highlights, and the lessons—I will be able to ignite a spark that will encourage you to find your strength, speak up when you finally have a seat at the table, define your nonnegotiables, and never lose sight of who you are along the way. I wish to inspire you to go from thinking you *could* to believing you *can* . . . believing in yourself and the power of possibility. And then rolling up your sleeves and getting to work to make it happen. If I could do it, so can you.

You hold the power within you to become your own superhero. You hold the power to change your life. Possibility is your superpower, a buoyant outlook is your sidekick, and your resolve and determination are what will drive you to push forward, jump over seemingly impossible hurdles, and run faster than the speed of light toward your dreams. Are you ready?

1

We Are All Potential

The Ancient One: "Do you wonder
what I see in your future?"
Dr. Strange: "No . . . Yes."
The Ancient One: "I never saw your
future, only its possibilities."

—DOCTOR STRANGE (2016)

We are all born into this world with potential—the potential to be whoever we desire to become and do whatever we set out to accomplish. My mother was the first one to imbue me with this power of possibility. Whenever I came to her to ask if I could do something, her answer was "If it has been done, you can do it. But if it hasn't been done, you should." With that phrase, she unknowingly gifted me with one of my most important driving forces in my life—it propelled that little girl to always consider the possibilities before her as something doable and attainable, no matter how outlandish they might have seemed to others.

❮ ❮ ❮

I was born in 1965 into a middle-class family in La Plata, Argentina, capital of the province of Buenos Aires, home to Argentina's largest cathedral, and known as the city of diagonal streets, which are lined with linden trees and bustling with students. As a little girl, I couldn't sit still. My parents could leave my sister sleeping in her crib just fine, but when I came along eighteen months later, all I did was wiggle around like a little worm, eyes wide open, taking in every inch of my surroundings—some things never change. I was born with an innate and bottomless curiosity that remains a big part of who I am today. As soon as I learned to talk, I began to ask questions, which my parents patiently answered. My thirst for knowledge was and continues to be insatiable.

My mother held a high-ranking position at the Ministry of Education, and my father was a psychologist and college professor. With two erudite parents, specializing in education, no less, it wasn't a question of whether my older sister and I would go to college when we grew up, but which college we'd attend. Other than the relative novelty of having two working parents in the sixties, we led a pretty run-of-the-mill middle-class life. There was never a day when we worried about how we could afford our next meal or whether our parents' paychecks would make it to the end of the month—everything was calm, almost predictable.

Until it wasn't.

When I was seven years old, my dad was diagnosed with lung cancer. He was forty years old. The doctor said they would have to remove a small piece of one of his lungs to give him a fighting chance. He scheduled the resection surgery but kept the whole ordeal to himself. On the day of his operation, my mom got a call at work.

"Hello, Mrs. Alonso. We need someone to drive your husband home."

"Home from where?" she asked, taken aback.

"From the hospital. He can't go home alone after his surgery."

Thunderstruck, she dropped everything and headed straight to the hospital.

The doctors said his surgery had gone well, so he was instructed to rest and avoid strenuous activities as he recovered. But a few days later, while at home following the doctor's orders, he suffered a stroke and passed away. Just like that.

One minute he was here—the next, he was gone.

I've blocked my memory of that day, that week, that year. Some people have the ability to absorb the events of their life like a sponge and recall the most minute detail of a moment that unfolded decades earlier. Not me. I have never been able to linger in the past—perhaps because of this explosive turning point in my life. I only recall my father's face because of the few pictures I have of him, but the rest is blurred by the shock of that sudden loss. I don't think we ever get over the death of a parent, especially at such a young age. I believe we simply learn how to live with the pain that enormous gap leaves behind. A pain that, with time, becomes an infrequent visitor, remaining mostly at bay yet, once in a while, showing up uninvited at our doorstep, unfurling that which we'd hoped to leave buried and in peace.

When my dad died, the trauma erased my tears. I was aware of the profound gap he left behind, yet I made a monumental effort to be a happy kid. Somehow, consciously or not, I figured out how to prevent the overwhelming sadness from invading my days. At that very early age, I learned how to compartmentalize my feelings, my life. I honestly don't think I could carry out my job now if I didn't know how to sort out the events of the day into boxes. Regardless of what happens on set, in the cutting room, at the office, or in my life, the show really must go on. People count on me to get results, so I need to carry with me a clear under-standing that many of the things that are said and done on the job that I could take personally are not about me at all. This is one of the bigger lessons I've learned from working with so many men throughout the years. Many of them have an uncanny ability to detach from the emotions of a moment and keep moving forward as if whatever happened wasn't such a big deal. But, from my personal experience, this behavior can sometimes come across as cold, bordering on hurtful, so I choose to detach with love. I consistently aim to take the path of kindness and fairness, no matter the circumstances. I don't always succeed, but it certainly makes a difference to try. Sometimes even the smallest conscious effort to stay kind can turn a volatile situation into a meaningful conversation.

❝ ❝ ❝

I've always had a grounded sense of what's right and wrong. The first time I recall standing up for this feeling is on the playground of my elementary school when some kids started teasing a girl in my class. At first it seemed like a fleeting moment of insolence, but as the minutes dragged on, it began to escalate into outright bullying. They began to deride her by spewing nasty epithets about her being Jewish. As I watched this unfold, overcome by the wrongness of it all, I shot over to the group and defiantly said, "Hey, what are you doing?" They quickly paused the verbal bashing and turned to look at me. "If you're saying that to her, it's like you're saying it to me," I declared unwaveringly. Even though I wasn't Jewish myself, her pain was so vivid I could feel it in my bones, and all I wanted to do was take it away. After mumbling a few weak excuses, they stopped and walked away.

No one should be teased or bullied for who they are, and if a group is willing to do this to one person, then it's only a matter of time before they turn and do it to someone else. Yet if we dare to raise our voices whenever possible, we can help put a stop to this type of nonsense—or at the very least bring a new wave of awareness to it—before it mushrooms into something beyond measure.

After my father died, I appeared happy and sure of myself, fighting for what was right in the little ways I could, yet a thunderous cloud had rolled into my heart, obscuring me from my emotions. Outwardly I could function just fine, but I had completely shut down on the inside. Because of this, the details of my life in the following years are murky, mere Polaroid snapshots in an album of momentous occasions with nothing really tying them together.

Meanwhile, as I tried to figure out how to keep on living without my dad, Argentina began to unravel before our eyes, entering its darkest chapter since becoming an independent nation in 1816. Things were heating up on the streets. The Montoneros—a left-wing militant fighting group founded by President Juan Domingo Perón during his second term in office, before he was overthrown by a military coup and exiled to Paraguay—turned on Perón for forming alliances with right-wing groups upon his return to Argentina and the start of his third term as president. It was a pretty volatile time, incensed by violence spawned from both sides of the political spectrum. And we, as citizens, were caught in the cross fire—until March 24, 1976, the day it all came to a screeching halt. By then, Juan Domingo Perón had passed away, and his widow, Isabel Perón, had taken office two years earlier. On that day in March, Argentina suffered its sixth and last military coup to date, the bloodiest and most horrifying of them all. It marked the beginning of what is now known as the Dirty War, which was relentlessly waged for the next seven years against left-wing political opponents, their families, and any suspected acquaintances. This atrocious period in Argentina's history claimed the lives of around thirty thousand people, many of whom were captured by the military and never heard from again—they became known as the "disappeared."

I was only ten years old on that fateful day. President Isabel Perón was overthrown by a military junta led by the infamous lieutenant general Jorge Rafael Videla. At three in the morning, TV and radio stations across the country were interrupted by the dreaded military march and the following announcement:

> *People are advised that as of today, the country is under the operational control of the Joint Chiefs General of the Armed Forces. We recommend to all residents strict compliance with the provisions and directives emanating from the military, security, or police authorities, and to be extremely careful to avoid individual or group actions and attitudes that may require drastic intervention from the operating personnel.*

As faint as my memory of those years can be, this is one moment that will be forever burned into my brain. My mom turned to my sister and me that morning and said, "This is not a good day." She paused, took a deep breath, and added, "From now on, you're going to have to look over your shoulder more often and be extra careful." Martial law was declared, and a curfew was put into effect immediately. "Just mind your own business," she said, emphasizing that the military was out for blood and wouldn't think twice about killing anyone who went against them.

Ten years earlier, during the country's previous coup d'état, General Juan Carlos Onganía had overthrown elected president Arturo Umberto Illia and risen to power as a military dictator whose goal was to establish a permanent authoritarian state.

One of Onganía's first orders of business was to revoke academic freedom and brutally end the autonomy of Argentina's public universities. Then followed the repression on the streets, which tagged women wearing miniskirts and men with long hair, as well as all avant-garde movements, as immoral. One day, amid this upheaval, my mom was walking home with me in her arms—I was almost one year old—when a gang of goons pulled up by the curb and burst out of their car yelling, "¡Viva Perón!" "¡Viva Evita!" My mom pulled my little body tighter into her thudding chest and fixed her gaze on the sidewalk, trying not to draw attention to us, but the goons took her actions and refusal to join in the chants as a slight against them and an act of complete disrespect. In a matter of seconds, the angry mob surrounded her, and their deafening shouts suddenly escalated into blows. As they furiously whacked her small frame, she curved over my body to protect me until she collapsed to the ground, drops of blood pooling on the stone pavers. The men scrambled into their car and sped away, not knowing if she was dead or alive. And now here we were, a decade later, with another authoritarian government in motion, churning up buried fears my mom had hoped she'd never have to experience again.

As we left for school the next morning, there was an eerie atmosphere to the seemingly normal day. While we went about our routines, military were deployed to patrol the streets and arrest political activists, unionists, students, and any other dissidents they came across. Come nightfall hundreds of people had been abducted. And this was only the beginning. Once the military junta officially took control a few days later, they seized power over state and municipal governments and established several covert detention camps where they jailed and tortured *anyone* they suspected might have ties to their opponents, which more often than not resulted in death.

My mom was terrified by word on the street of what was really happening clandestinely with the military dictatorship, but she had to put on her best poker face. As a high-ranking official in the Ministry of Education, a government body, and dean of the city's public university, she now had to work alongside military officers every day. While at home, behind closed doors, she fed us strength and urged us to think for ourselves with an open mind, out in this new reality she had to do her best to remain as neutral as possible to keep us safe. And she did it all alone, as a single mother and a widow.

From 1976 to 1981, everyone kept to themselves, trying to stay alive or quietly favoring the heightened—albeit false—sense of restored peace and order. It was an unsettling time, almost like living with an abuser, fearing what could happen if you didn't comply. The military dictatorship portrayed to the world that they were fighting for a cause, waging a civil war for the good of the country, protecting us from future harm. But back at home, the truth was a different story. People were being wrongfully incarcerated, tortured, raped, murdered, and "disappeared." At first, the military were operating in deep stealth mode, diligently covering their tracks. So, for a while, the days and weeks chugged along like any other year, until the military began to get sloppy and overconfident. That's when pieces of that rumored under-world began to surface here and there, showing us point-blank the danger lurking just under our noses.

One day, the military stormed into my classroom, seized our teacher, and dragged him out by the hair. We never saw him again. A short time later, they did it again to another teacher. With time, we even heard whispers of classmates whose siblings had "disappeared." It was like coming face-to-face with the monster we knew had been hiding under the bed, the one the government tried to convince us wasn't real. Yet as kids, even though no one dared voice it at first, many of us could sense that something bleak was brewing. We were like sitting ducks. If someone you happened to know was captured and tortured, after getting their teeth and nails pulled or being raped repeatedly it was only a matter of time until they caved and shared a few names to find respite from the continuous torment. It wasn't just a chance connection with a suspected dissident that could screw you over; even an inkling of dissent could be your undoing. A man having long hair, a woman dressing like a hippie, or anyone simply being at the wrong place at the wrong time during a raid could land that person in jail. And there was no "innocent until proven guilty." Once they had their hands on you, the only verdict was guilty as charged. It took us a few years to wake up to the truth behind this wretched reality.

All I remember thinking is *There's something awfully wrong with what they're doing.* If you have differing political ideas from the standing government, you should have the freedom to voice them without being under the threat of losing your life and without feeling the need to express yourself through violence. That belief in fairness, in doing the right thing, began to grow within me, and, as the years passed, I latched on to it as my beacon of hope: Hope for the wrongs to one day finally be righted. Hope to feel free in my own country. Hope to express my beliefs without consequences. And yes, hope for a better tomorrow.

❆ ❆ ❆

No matter where we start or what we experience, whether we are marked as being strong or weak, big or small, fast or slow, the potential to fight for what we believe in, to battle what holds us back, lies within us all. Our origins don't determine our fate because we are all born with innate potential and the power to choose what we do with it. Think about your favorite superheroes and their origin stories. They come from vastly different backgrounds: from the humble beginnings in New York of Captain America—whose father died in World War I before he was born, leaving his mother, a nurse, to raise him, until she succumbed to tuberculosis, leaving him orphaned by the age of eighteen—to Captain Marvel's 1960s Boston upbringing by working class parents who tried to pigeonhole her into stereotypical female roles, to heirs to the throne like Thor and Black Panther who seemingly had it all since birth. Their origins informed their identities, motivations, and insecurities, yet what eventually turned them into superheroes was neither their circumstances nor where they came from but the ability to harness their will and tap into their potential to be their best selves.

Yes, we are born into a certain life, family, environment.

That's why I am not just my mother and father's daughter; I am also the daughter of Argentina's most secretive and harrowing military dictatorship, as well as a seven-year-old girl who lost her father way too soon. But what I choose to do with all of that, where I have chosen to go from there, has always been up to me.

2

It's Not About
What We've Lost;
It's About What
We Have Left

**"We lost friends. We lost family.
We lost a part of ourselves.
Today, we have a chance to take it all back."**

—CAPTAIN AMERICA, *AVENGERS: ENDGAME* (2019)

The roads we travel from the moment we come into this world are punctuated by gaps and craters. Our challenge as the years march on is to remain focused on what we have left rather than what we've lost. To do that, I have found it helpful to figure out how to fill those gaps and craters. But what are they, exactly? How do we recognize them? The gaps can represent anything from lack of a job, to lack of understanding, lack of success, or lack of relationships. And the craters are larger holes in our lives such as the lack of fulfillment, the lack of love, the lack of identity, a life-altering event, or the loss of our loved ones—and part of ourselves in the process.

As Captain America says in the *Avengers: Endgame* scene in the HQ hangar while rallying his friends for the fight of their lives: "Most of us are going somewhere we know. That doesn't mean we should know what to expect." That's how the gaps and craters play out in our existence—we're usually in familiar territory when a blindsiding sinkhole appears at our feet. These are our defining moments: Either we will get sucked into that obscure vacuum, or we will manage to claw our way to safety and figure out how to deal with the situation, put the pieces back together, and move on.

Losing my father created a meteoric crater in my path that would mark the rest of my life. But I didn't let it define me. At first, I was in total denial. At school I used to talk about my dad as if he were still alive. My friends knew the truth, but they let me have this coping mechanism. I spent years without shedding a single tear—I buried my emotions deep in that crater and did everything in my power to stop that dark abyss from swallowing me whole. I instinctively began to fill the void by focusing on what I could control, addressing the nooks and crannies within my reach. Although I was only seven years old, I slapped a smile on my face, let my can-do spirit hold the fort, and unconsciously took on the role of the "responsible one" to keep our family unit running.

As the years passed and my sister metamorphosed from rambunctious little girl to defiant teen, I laced up my good-girl shoes extra tight and remained steadfast on that trustworthy path. I was a straight-A student who didn't make waves or cause trouble as a child and eagerly pitched in whenever I could to make my mom's life easier. By the time I was ten years old, I was already standing in line at the bank to deposit my mom's checks, then stopping by the market with my sister to get groceries for the three of us. As I write this, I look at my thirteen-year-old daughter now and can't even begin to imagine her running these types of errands. That's just not part of our reality today. But back in the 1970s, I didn't think twice about any of it.

The consistent feeling of being out of control in our society gave me such an intense sense of powerlessness that it subconsciously forced me to seek harmony and balance in my daily life, and I took that to an extreme. My high school friends say that anytime they were in a bind, be it with another friend or at school, I was the first to notice and quietly intercede. And, under those circumstances, I usually managed to keep my cool, speaking to others with respect, carefully measuring my words to keep the peace, solve the issue, and move on. My family and friends were my everything and losing someone else was not an option, so I took control of whatever I could to make sure we all remained together and out of harm's way. I didn't plan to fill these gaps in my life. I did it out of necessity. I needed to feel less impotent. Call it resilience, perseverance, or whatever you might, I honestly don't know where it came from, but it was there, and it influenced how I continued to live my life from then on.

The craters in our lives don't just appear when we're young—though those oftentimes have the biggest impact. They can materialize at any given time. Our lives are like a wheel of Swiss cheese. We have stretches that are smooth and sturdy, but our path is also dotted with unexpected holes. Interestingly, cheese makers call these holes in Swiss cheese eyes. The specific bacteria added to the cheese that create these eyes also give Swiss cheese its signature nutty flavor profile. What's more, if there's a wheel of Swiss cheese that doesn't have eyes, it's considered defective. In other words, the gaps and craters in our lives, although difficult to traverse, are what make us the unique, complex, and complete humans we are today. If we're willing to pay attention, they will teach us some of the most important lessons of our lives. And they can fuel us with the strength to overcome future holes. When you address the gaps in your life, you open yourself up to your ultimate superpower: possibility.

€ € €

Growing up without a father in a turmoil-filled country under military rule, with few options for advancement within reach, didn't stop me from imagining more. Possibility was my beacon of hope. And when I found out, through classmates, that our school was participating in the Pacific Intercultural Exchange program that sent students to the United States for six months, my heart leaped. A chance to escape my fear-filled land, experience another country, and quench my incessant curiosity? Yes, please! That evening, I went straight to my mom with this opportunity.

"Sure, you can go," she said.

A rush of joy flushed my cheeks.

". . . if you figure out how to pay for it yourself," she added, likely thinking that at fourteen there was no way in hell I'd be able to come up with the three thousand dollars for the round-trip flight and six-month stay up north.

I let out a big sigh, but all hope was not lost. My mom never crushed my requests with an outright no. She never resorted to the parent classics: "No, this is what you're going to do." "No, this is what you have to study." "No, you cannot travel abroad as a teenager." Her go-to was the "yes, but" strategy: "Sure, you can do that, but you have to figure out how to do it." I think she probably thought things would end there. But rather than give up, I took it as a challenge.

Ask anyone who knows me or has worked with me: To this day, no is not an option I take lightly. Part of living in possibility is knowing that there are doors that will be shut with an outright no. But it's up to us to find another way. I don't want to sit in a conference room and waste precious time rattling out an exhausting list of all the things we *can't* do to tell a story. When I find myself in that situation, I make it my mission to shift the perspective in the room to focus on what is currently within our reach, on what we can do right now to move the project forward. With that approach, the "can't-do" list becomes background noise, and this allows us to clear the path to discovering other ways of dealing with those gaps to get to our destination. At the end of the day, your no will be my yes . . . eventually.

❝ ❝ ❝

By putting this first "yes, but" hurdle in front of me, my mom unwittingly kicked my entrepreneurial can-do spirit into perpetual high gear. At fourteen I didn't have many ways to earn three thousand dollars. It wasn't like I could go get a job at some shop. So after racking my brain, I thought, *Key chains!* I had recently made a round of handmade wooden beaded key chains with my friend Vivi, and they had sold well. Since they were a small item, I knew I'd likely have a better chance at placing them in stores. And everyone used them.

Light bulb moment: check.

But what if I stepped it up a notch? I decided to design my key chains in the shape of a swim fin.

Design: check.

To net the three thousand dollars I needed for my trip, I calculated that I would have to make one thousand key chains and sell them at a little over three dollars each to cover the cost of manufacturing and reach my savings goal.

Budget: check.

I went to a local ironsmith who had the necessary equipment and explained my plan and how much I could afford to pay him for the key chains, which were easy to make.

Negotiation: check.

And this man, who had never met me before but thought it was beautiful to dream and travel, believed in me and said yes—God bless his faith in me!

Manufacturer: check.

I gave the ironsmith my little stash of savings to cover his materials and planned to pay the rest of his fee with the money I made from selling these key chains. This way he wouldn't be at a loss and I wouldn't owe anyone any money, which was an advantageous starting point. I figured it would take me about four weeks to make back my investment with a profit.

As soon as the ironsmith delivered the one thousand key chains in all the colors of the rainbow, I walked straight over to La Plata's most bustling, well-known commercial street: Calle 8. That was the spot back in the day, the place to meet up with friends at a café, do some window-shopping, or catch a movie at one of the theaters. There were so many big and small stores and so much foot traffic that I knew if I was going to sell my key chains anywhere, it would be here. I knocked on every viable door, showed shop owners my merchandise, and asked if I could leave them on consignment in their window display. The key chains were bright and colorful, which made them stand out in every window where they were placed. I must've left around ten or twenty pieces in each shop, together with my landline number—there were no cell phones back then. Within a few days, our phone began ringing off the hook. The key chains were flying off the shelves. By week three, I had sold out my inventory and paid the ironsmith, and I approached my mom one evening with my earnings.

"Mom, I have the money. Could you please buy my ticket now?" I said as I placed the bills on the dining room table.

Gobsmacked, her jaw dropped. "Where did you get this money, Victoria? Who did you get it from?" she said, worry furrowing her brow.

"No, no, I earned it," I said and went on to explain my enterprise.

"And how did you come up with that idea?" she asked, still astonished by the feat her fourteen-year-old daughter had managed to accomplish on her own.

I paused for a second. I hadn't initially told her my plan, fearing she might not support it. "I guess I figured it would serve as a good filler for the shops' display windows, plus they are inexpensive, and colorful enough to catch the attention of passersby," I replied, in hopes that she'd focus on my successful outcome. "It was a crazy idea, but it worked."

My mom nodded along, seemingly still unsure of where that ingenuity had originated. Then she said, "Maybe it worked because you didn't doubt yourself." And, true to her word, she helped me register for the exchange program and bought my ticket.

Instead of giving up and wallowing over the hurdle in my path, her "yes, but" pushed me to consider the possibility, take the chance, and fill the monetary gap.

❬ ❬ ❬

A few years ago, while giving a talk inspired by the phrase you see on London subway platforms, MIND THE GAP, I suddenly said to the crowd, "You know what? We shouldn't just mind the gap. . . . We should fill it. That's how I got here. I filled the gaps others didn't want to undertake. I took on all the jobs that others turned down." That night, I began to ruminate on this phrase. *Filling the gap* wasn't just a way of working—it was a way of being.

In my case, it started with me as a kid feeling the need to fill the emotional gap in my family. I aimed to be supportive and took on responsibilities that shouldn't have fallen on my shoulders, just to quell the chaos. What began as a survival tactic eventually became a default mode of operation that taught me to be resourceful and created a problem solver out of me, laying the essential groundwork for what I would later need to embark on my career as a producer. My beacon of possibility and hard work had now opened the door to the exchange program in 1981, my first trip abroad, my first visit to the United States, six months in San Diego, California—a catalyst that would eventually change the course of my life.

I knew nothing of San Diego. Since there was no Google back then to quickly look places up, my mom and I sat down at our kitchen table and thought about the people we knew who had traveled to the United States. We recalled all the stories about New York's skyscrapers, Miami's beaches, and Orlando's Disney World, typical destinations for Argentines at the time, but none of our friends had made the trek to California. So I turned to the lyrics of the Mamas & the Papas' "California Dreamin'" and smiled, realizing I would be in a place where the sun warmed the streets in winter. This was further confirmed by the West Coast sunshine mentioned in the Beach Boys' "California Girls." No complaints on my end; to this day I do better in warmer climates. My family spent our summers at the nearby beaches along the Atlantic, so I was also thrilled by the chance to experience the Pacific Ocean for the first time, and don't even get me started on the surfers. *Swoon!* And when it came to imagining the school, my mind went straight to *Grease*, which had hit theaters a couple of years earlier. That's all I knew about the US educational system—the rest I would discover on my own.

In retrospect, I realize that I didn't just set this plan in motion to participate in that exchange program; I also did it because I needed to continue dealing with the craters in my life. I was weaving a net that would prevent me from being devoured by them, so that I could look to the future instead of the past. It's like what Captain America says in *Avengers: Endgame* during a group meeting for those dealing with life and grief after Thanos's snap: "That's great. You did the hardest part. You took the jump; you didn't know where you were gonna come down. And that's it. That's those little brave baby steps you gotta take. To try and become whole again. To try and find purpose."

❮ ❮ ❮

Think about any of the times you've hit a hurdle, roadblock, or crater in your life. When you fell, what did you choose to do to become whole again? Did you pull yourself back up on your own? How? What skills or strengths helped you? The answers to these questions might reveal the tools that already live within you, the ones you need to survive your darkest nights. I've done a lot of soul-searching and I honestly don't have a formula for you to follow because it's a uniquely personal process. Some people need to lean on their circle of support, and others, like me, feel the need to get to work, repair the gap, and charge forward. There's no right or wrong way, so long as you're doing something about it and not abandoning yourself.

Let's go back to Dr. Strange. He was at the top of his game as a surgeon, an incredibly talented yet cocky man, when he injured and permanently damaged his most prized possession: his hands. Yet the moment he decided to let go of what he had lost and focus on what he could do with what he had left, he wholeheartedly entered the world of mystic arts and became the most powerful sorcerer in existence. The roads vary, but the end goal is pretty much the same for all of us, both superheroes and humans alike: Process and understand the past, fill the gaps in your life, and set your eyes on the future. That is where possibility lives.

Arriving in San Diego, California, at fifteen years of age was almost like landing on another planet. I went from the underlying fear and repressive streets of a military dictatorship to the freewheeling life of sunny California in the early eighties, and my eyes were popping out of their sockets. The towering palm trees against the vivid blue sky, the warmth of the incandescent sun, the outline of rolling hills in the distance. I drank it all up as we drove to my host family's house. This was where I would be living for the next six months—I just couldn't believe it.

I was assigned an all-American family that was very welcoming and accommodating, but, even though my reading and writing skills in English were in great shape—most schools in Argentina teach English, starting in elementary school—there was still a language barrier, and it was quite frustrating. You don't realize how much more you have to learn until you're in a room with native speakers. The first time I said "I can't wait to go to the bitch," my host family almost fell out of their seats laughing. I just stared back at them, slightly bemused and hurt. *Why are they laughing at me?* I thought. "Wait, what did I say wrong?" I asked. That's when I learned that the right pronunciation for a word I had read hundreds of times was *beach*.

As the weeks passed, my ears slowly grew used to the different drawls, accents, pronunciation styles, and slang, though the word *ain't* continued to trip me up. My instinct was to stay true to the grammar I had so diligently learned back home in school, so I just couldn't wrap my head around why the kids at this school would say *ain't* instead of *am not* or *are not*. Then it hit me: Grammar didn't really matter as much as actually being able to reach the other person, to communicate, connect, and bond through a common language, even if it's not perfectly spoken in either case—them with their slang, and me with my mispronunciations. We talked funny but we got along, and that's all that mattered. For the record, I still talk funny to this day and have never been able to pronounce the word *hippopotamus* without tripping over the syllables!

What really blew my mind wide open during those six months was the school. At home in my strict, military-style school, the designated attire was a crisp white uniform with a skirt that hit below the knee, blue or black socks, and brown penny loafers. Makeup was out of the question, hair had to be worn up in a tight ponytail secured by a blue or white band or ribbon, and the only jewelry that could adorn our ears was pearl earrings. If we dared break with this rigid dress code, we'd immediately get a demerit and a scolding for each act of rebellion. Now imagine that same fifteen-year-old girl stepping into a public high school in San Diego in 1981 on her first day of school in the United States wearing the subdued colors she assumed were the norm. I felt I had been plopped into the middle of a fashion runway. The girls had neon-colored pants and off-the-shoulder tops with bold graphics, and the boys wore swim trunks and flip-flops and rolled up to school on their skateboards. Some kids drove in with surfboards saddled on their cars, ready to hit the waves as soon as the bell rang, signaling the day was over. It was early eighties beach life to the max. The megawatt makeup, overstated jewelry, tattoos ... I didn't even know what a tattoo was until I walked those school halls.

One of the extracurricular activities I decided to join was the drama club—my very first foray into the world of acting. The day I walked into the Mission Bay High School theater my jaw hit the floor. Rows of light wooden seats cascaded down to the ultra-modern stage where I would first experience the collaborative art form that would become a precursor to my decades-long career. My high school in La Plata, housed in a late nineteenth-century building where most of our school functions took place either in the assembly hall or on the outside patio, was completely dwarfed by the eight-hundred-seat theater before me. I quickly joined the rest of the members at the foot of the stage and proceeded to pay close attention to every word that came out of their mouths, eagerly trying to decipher the specific terms and phrases used in the theater world. Diving headfirst into a new activity in a language that was not my own was undoubtedly a struggle. Honestly, on a good day, if I understood half of what was said, I took it as a win. But it taught me that a smile can oftentimes be more valuable than a full vocabulary. So I smiled a lot!

While I was there I participated in one musical, *Hollywood Here I Come*, an adaptation of *A Chorus Line* that required a much larger production than what I was used to. When I was cast as one of the background chorus girls, I yearned to be put in the back row so that I could mask any screwups in the routine, but they kept placing me in the middle. I knew I could hold my own singing, but dancing? Well, let's just say I'm the quintessential dance-to-your-own-rhythm kind of person. I'm so terrible others avoid dancing with me because I can't keep time, yet instinctively I want to lead. I knew this was not the part for me, but I slipped into the red scoop-neck leotard with a white belted waist and a white bow on my chest, put on my Mary Jane heels, grabbed my white top hat, high-kicked my way across the stage, and gave it my best shot. My dance bit eventually became the humor in the scene! Like I said before, fill the gap!

Although I wasn't in my element with this specific role, I stuck it out because I enjoyed working with a group of people who loved the arts, and my curiosity always got the best of me. I wanted to learn why the director made certain choices over others. I wanted to learn how the choreographer thought of putting each of us in a certain spot to make the moves work seamlessly. I wanted to learn how the high school band figured out when to come in on a number—yes, we had live music! I wanted to learn the costume team's creative process. When one of my theater mates said, "Come on, Victoria, we have to do our makeup," I froze. "What?

I don't know how to do makeup. I don't wear makeup." And then I thought, *Wait a minute, here I am feeling petrified by not knowing how to apply mascara and only two months ago, I was petrified about disappearing under a military dictatorship!* So I figured it out. What I loved most about that experience was how seamlessly the different departments worked together to create a production that audience members could enjoy. We were all led by the need and desire to perform, and that performance held the sheer joy of doing something that we loved. Every aspect taught me something new and, although at times I felt I was out of my element, I thrived on the exposure to this new world and lapped it up. At night, I would lie in bed and ask myself, *Did you understand at least half of what was going on today?* My answer was usually yes, which inspired me to get up the next day and attempt to meander through the language barrier and theater codes all over again.

I was fifteen, and for the first time I was absorbing the normalcy of freedom of speech and self-expression. *Wow, these people really have it together,* I thought. They were gifted with the right to be who they were, they took full ownership of that right, and the school welcomed their varied identities. It was beyond my wildest dreams and I loved every second of it, even the hurdles, because it fell in line with my perspective and beliefs. A place where I could freely express who I was and what I believed, without terrifying consequences hanging over my head like a razor-sharp, jagged dagger—that felt like my place in the world.

By the time the program finished and I was to return home, a seed had been planted: I wanted that life. I had an urge to live differently, travel, and learn other languages, and it only grew from then on. I was weaving a new net now, one of hope and dreams for a better future, one filled with the power of possibility fueled by freedom, one that I was determined to return to . . . eventually.

❮ ❮ ❮

Superheroes also confront life-altering craters on their path, those moments of darkness teeming with obstacles and fear, those flashes of doubt that shake their foundation, but like Tony Stark says in *Avengers: Endgame*: "It's not about how much we lost. It's about how much we have left. We're the Avengers." And *you* are the avenger in your own life. It's up to you to face the craters that have impacted who you are and weave a mesh of growth that breaks your fall and allows you to climb out of the darkness, giving you the choice to reclaim your world of possibility. That's the essence of resilience, the will to pick yourself up and keep moving forward, regardless of the obstacles or naysayers holding you back—even if they do laugh a little when you dance.

3

There Is Strength in Your Weakness

**"I choose to run towards my problems,
and not away from them.
Because that's what heroes do."**

—THOR, *THOR: RAGNAROK* (2017)

Strong is good, weak is bad—that's the sentiment many of us have been fed throughout our lives. And sure, sometimes your strength will be your saving grace. But limitation is the mother of all creation. As film producer and Marvel Studios copresident Louis D'Esposito always said, when your strength is diminished, you're pushed to come up with alternative roads, new ideas that could give way to fresh possibilities. To which I add: Within that new possibility lies a life lesson that may not have entered your world had it not been for a moment of perceived weakness. This new perspective could also provide you with a different way to see your strength.

Think about Thor in *Thor: Ragnarok*. When he's cast away to the strange planet of Sakaar, Thor is captured by Valkyrie, who throws a small disc on his neck that renders him unconscious at the push of a button. Yet his capture, this moment of weakness, eventually leads to his reconnecting with Hulk—after their epic gladiator fight—making amends with Valkyrie, and joining forces with them both to return home to Asgard and defeat his sister, Hela. What's more, in that battle with his sister, she strikes his face and cuts his eye out, but this loss gifts him with a vision of his father, who reminds him that Asgard is not a place—Asgard is their people. These moments of weakness have one thing in common: They gave way to alternative circumstances and ideas, which eventually led to triumph. They allowed him to see his home and his family in a very different light and, because of this, he understood the true meaning of community.

Because the bulk of my career has been centered in the world of visual effects, which is all about computer-generated imagery (CGI), you might think I love computers. But guess what? I truly don't. I'm not naturally computer savvy. That trait could be considered one of my weaknesses in the field of visual effects. As the years have rolled on, I have often wondered *why* I don't like computers. If I am truly honest with myself, I don't like them because I don't understand them. It's that simple. Most of us are inclined to do that which comes easily to us. If you ask me to choose between fencing or tennis, I'll choose tennis blindfolded because

I've played that sport since I was a kid. On the other hand, I've never tried fencing, I don't know how it works, and I'm not sure I would be any good at it. But maybe, if I gave it a shot and put in the hours, I could end up liking it too.

That's why I always make a point to prioritize what I don't know how to do. My curiosity has always balanced out my weaknesses. I'm consistently learning new things; it's what nourishes my mind and creativity. Then, as I dig into what I don't know, I slowly fall in love with it, and all I want to do is know more, more, more. I am not and never was the one writing code or operating the software that creates the beautiful, jaw-dropping computer graphics in our movies—I still don't quite get how some of those programs work—but I've learned to understand enough to know our limitations and how much an artist can contribute to our storytelling. By knowing how something is done, I am able to nourish, protect, and support our project and those working on it.

One example of this happened to me at Marvel Studios. When I first signed on to work on *Iron Man*, I did it because it was going to be shot in Los Angeles, which was my nonnegotiable at the time—we'll get into more of this key point later—but growing up I never liked superheroes. I was never a fan. I wasn't eagerly awaiting the next Superman movie or the next episode of *The Incredible Hulk* or *Wonder Woman*, even though she was a total hit at the time. I never read any of the comics either. My only go-to comic strip was Quino's *Mafalda*, featuring a six-year-old girl who reflected on the state of the world and humanity by way of incredibly relatable, poignant, and truthful observations that resonated across all age groups.

Mafalda was and will always be my superhero. Through *Mafalda*, its author, Quino, didn't focus on political commentary—although there was some of that. Rather, he aimed to express universal feelings of freedom, loyalty, and family, as well as a consistent aversion to soup. Mafalda has always been my freedom, my voice, my way, my light. I remember reading those comics and thinking, *I want to meet her!* I admired her audacity, and I loved how she questioned everything and silenced adults with her simple yet incisive thoughts on life. Mafalda was wise beyond her years.

In one strip, her mother is heading out the door and tells Mafalda not to open the door to absolutely anyone, no matter how insistently they knock. Mafalda agrees, and her mother shuts the door and is walking into the elevator when Mafalda pops out and says, "Mom! But what if it's happiness?"

Of course, I thought, *why wouldn't you open the door to happiness?* What a beautiful and timeless message to receive at any age. Those universal themes that I absorbed as a kid through *Mafalda* are what I have tried to help weave into our Marvel shows and movies.

I have often been asked why I helped make more than thirty superhero films if I don't like the genre. This led me to ask myself a similar question: *Why am I not into superheroes?* After mulling this over for a while, I finally landed on a simple answer: Because I didn't find them relatable as a kid. I didn't wear a cape or have a shield or a hammer, and, although I really yearned for this, I couldn't fly. I didn't look like the superheroes, and I knew for sure that I couldn't save the world. But I did look like Mafalda when I was little. We were both round and fluffy, and I could easily identify with her thoughts and emotions. Mafalda wasn't solving the world's problems, but day in and day out, she challenged the status quo. She was the epitome of *truth to power*. So, if I was going to help my colleagues tell superhero stories, I needed to find a way to relate to those characters, as I did with Mafalda, so that others like me could do the same. One of the reasons I immediately clicked with Tony Stark was that although he is incredibly smart, he is also a flawed human being, like the rest of us. As I dug into his story and discovered how he chooses to pivot his talent and intellect from creating weapons of war to doing good, I found a clear and relatable link to that character, and I was hooked.

From that day forward and throughout the years, that connection with the characters and the plot was the key feedback I consistently brought to the table. If I was watching a scene or an action sequence and it wasn't doing it for me, I would not mince words: "I don't necessarily care about this." I wanted to care. I wanted us to make adjustments so that we all cared about what was happening on the screen, so that we could all relate to, at the very least, one line, one gesture, one scene beyond the action and effects. If a scene was not moving the film forward in any way and not making us like the character more—or less—I would poke at it to see if we could either improve it or do without it. And so, at Marvel, the apparent weakness of me not liking superheroes became one of my greatest strengths because it pushed me to consistently suggest we make these all-powerful beings more human, more relatable. And this, in turn, brought a fresh take to the table. There it is again—the strength in a weakness, the power of possibility in full display.

€ € €

When I think of weakness on a personal level, the first image that comes to mind is the early eighties in Argentina. During the first few years after the military coup of 1976, the de facto government continued to maintain that they were fighting a civil war. Though it became increasingly apparent this was not the case, the fear was palpable on the streets, and no one dared speak up, terrified they too might one day cease to exist. But as civil rights violations grew and the human rights association Mothers of the Plaza de Mayo began to hold weekly vigils in front of the Casa Rosada, which houses the president's office, demanding to know where their disappeared children had gone, they drew international attention to their cause. This, in turn, inspired more people at home to defy the military-inflicted terror and raise their voices against the atrocities that were happening in our country. Despite the imposed curfews and censorship, by 1980 more people had begun to organize and participate in political demonstrations protesting the dictatorship. Enough was enough.

As I watched all these events begin to unfold, I took a keen interest in the political justice system; the sense of right and wrong only grew stronger within me as I moved through my adolescence and experienced freedom of expression during the exchange program in California. Fairness. That's what I was after.

My mom, terrified of ruffling the wrong feathers at work, continued to put her head down and mind her own business, focused on keeping my sister and me fed and out of harm's way. Up until then, I had done my best to not cause her any troubles. I knew she had a lot to deal with as the head of our household, raising two daughters on her own. So I didn't disobey my mother, and I always told her where I was, but when the marches began to take place in La Plata, I felt a deep-seated need to participate, to freely express my beliefs, regardless of the dangers doing so could incur.

Now we know that the highest rate of disappearances during the military dictatorship happened in La Plata. It was also home to some of the abysmal, now infamous, clandestine detention centers where prisoners were tortured, raped, and oftentimes murdered, not to mention the setting of the ghastly Noche de los Lápices (Night of the Pencils). That appalling event began on the night of September 16, 1976, only a few months after the fateful coup that put the military in power and gave way to the dissolution of political parties, the end of all national congressional sessions, and the persecution of all opponents of the military dictatorship. Ten high school students were kidnapped and tortured by the dictatorship that night because they were considered part of a potentially subversive group, and only four lived to tell the tale.

As some of these horrifying details began to reach me in underground gatherings and by word of mouth over the years, I just kept thinking, *We have to take risks; otherwise, why are we here?* So, together with a couple of my friends who were also activists at heart, I began to join as many protests as I could to help pump up the volume of our collective voice. I was only sixteen years old.

At every march, there were always a few people standing on the front lines, holding the large banners that demanded answers. I was one of those people proudly lifting my voice and carrying our message down our city streets. But one day, halfway through the march, my arms gave in to the weight of the signage, so I asked someone to take over for me. Giving my muscles a rest, I slowed my pace and fell back into the crowd behind the banner, never missing a beat with the chants. Then it happened. Gunshots. Chaos. Men and women with bullet wounds plummeting to the ground in front of me. Running for cover. Heart pounding. Blood curdling. The military had opened fire on the peaceful protestors. Whenever this happened, they shot to kill.

If I'd had the strength to continue carrying that banner, I might not be around today to share my story. Yet this incident didn't break my spirit; it didn't stop me. I didn't take it as a warning sign to retreat for my own good. If anything, it only fired me up further and made me want to stand up in the name of those we had lost and participate in even more protests and gatherings. We might not have had the physical strength to fight the military, but we did have our voices, and as the years progressed, we gathered more courage and made ourselves heard. Casualties were part of the risk, and I was ready to risk it all.

❮ ❮ ❮

As if what we were going through as a country wasn't enough, on April 2, 1982, in a clear political move, the military dictatorship decided to invade the Islas Malvinas (Falkland Islands), a British colony located about three hundred miles east of southern Argentina, ultimately inciting a war with Great Britain, home to one of the most powerful armed forces in the world. The military junta believed that winning back the Falkland Islands would help bring the Argentine people together in one patriotic fell swoop and make them forget about the human rights abuses we had been suffering for the previous six years and counting. And at first, it seemed like their plan was off to a good start.

People immediately took to the streets on that fateful day to celebrate this military maneuver. I was almost carried away by the patriotic sentiment of defending what was rightfully ours myself until my mom stopped me short and said, "There's nothing to celebrate here. Today is not a good day for our country." She was right, and those words have remained etched in my brain and heart. What I didn't know at sixteen that I understand now is that no one wins in war. The soldiers who were sent to fight were eighteen- and nineteen-year-old kids who didn't have the proper training and didn't even know how to handle the foreign weapons they were handed to defend themselves. Worst of all, the de facto government assumed Great Britain's response would be tepid at best, with room for negotiations—they never anticipated that within a month, our ten thousand soldiers would have to confront Great Britain's twenty-five thousand soldiers armed to the teeth on land, sea, and air. By the end of the short-lived seventy-four-day confrontation, more than 1,200 Argentine soldiers had suffered injuries and 649 had died. The military junta's plan had backfired tremendously, yet our collective power as a people only grew stronger.

During those excruciating weeks, a student committee had been formed at my school to help put together care packages for our soldiers. Naturally, those with the need to do something more joined in, which meant the school had inadvertently created an ideal meeting spot for student activists to quietly network and share knowledge of the unspoken atrocities happening on our city blocks. Meanwhile, aside from going to the marches, I also began to attend nightly clandestine gatherings in the Bachillerato de Bellas Artes basement to hear the Mothers of the Plaza de Mayo speak. I wanted to know what was really happening. I had tasted freedom of expression and political views in San Diego; I didn't want to live in the dark anymore.

Around the same time, some of my friends and I decided to join forces to reactivate our school's student center, which had been shut down when the dictatorship rose to power. We had spent the last four years enduring constant repression at school—everything from the policing of how we dressed to the banning of books in our literature classes and the restriction of any mention of politics or democratic systems in our civics classes. And we had witnessed persecution firsthand: The school director and principal had ties with the military and on more than one occasion had reported faculty members who later disappeared. All we wanted was to have a voice and real representation at school again. The center was finally inaugurated in 1984, once democracy was restored. Even though we weren't there to use it ourselves—we had already graduated by then—it remains part of our student legacy.

❦ ❦ ❦

Sure, I was protesting and fiercely fighting for our rights any way I could, trying to take down a system that was killing people, but I was also a sixteen-year-old girl weak in the knees from a crush and yearning to find some semblance of normalcy amid the transgressions we were up against. When I found out that my crush had joined a local independent theater group, Teatro La Lechuza, along with some of my closest friends, I decided to explore acting once again just to be closer to all of them. Amid such turbulence, family and friendships were the grounding force that cradled our torn-up spirits.

That year, the group was putting on a play titled *Asaltaron a doña Nuez* (Doña Nuez Got Mugged). I was cast as one of the two leads—the thieves who mug Doña Nuez—and my best friend, Alejo García Pintos, was the good kid who brought us to justice. At first, our weekly rehearsals were a place to hang out with my friends, flirt with my crush, and let my guard down, hidden away from the outside chaos. I'd never had the urgency or desire to be an actor as a kid. Instead, I wanted to be a veterinarian; I wanted to be surrounded by animals. Since then I have adopted more than thirteen rescued dogs over the years. But when this possibility to act presented itself, I said yes. I had no idea if I'd be good at it. I just had a weakness for a boy, that so-called weakness opened a door I had never seriously considered before, and I walked through it to see what was on the other side. Ever since then, I've always been open to what is presented along my path.

As the weeks went by, I really started to get into the play and began to connect with the backstage work too. After experiencing the Mission Bay High School drama club, I understood far more about props, costumes, lighting, music, and sound, and I was eager to use these skills at La Lechuza. Sure, I had gone from an 800-seat theater to one that could hold 120 people at maximum capacity, but this wasn't part of a school. This was an actual independent theater that needed to sell tickets and draw a crowd. So I started to ask questions about their marketing and publicity, everything from ticket pricing and selling concessions to how they advertised their productions. I absorbed every tidbit of information like a parched sponge—to this day, I remain fascinated by the process of creating something from nothing, be it a play, a movie, or a book. Before I knew it, this activity had gone beyond liking a boy or wanting to hang out with my crew. I was bitten by the theater bug, and it bit me hard.

Acting has never been my strong suit—I couldn't for the life of me remember my lines—but it was the only way I knew how to tell stories and express myself in this art form, so I forged ahead. With time I came to realize that those months in the theater saved my life. I truly believe it. This newly discovered passion required time and dedication, and despite the emotional push and pull between the fight on the streets and the safety in the theater, I didn't let the cause take over my life. I got invited to several protests and I said yes to as many as my courage allowed me to attend. If I felt unsafe or had a bad feeling or had a rehearsal or performance, then I wouldn't go. This meant that on the days when I chose the theater over going to a march, I was ultimately protected from several casualty-ridden demonstrations. I knew in my heart that I gave those protests my all when I attended, standing in the front rows and defiantly raising my voice in our fight for democracy, so I allowed myself the choice to also do what I loved and what made me happy. That space and time became my refuge.

The first time I worked on a movie soundstage, I thought, *Wait, I've been here before.* The fresh smell of wood, the camaraderie, the hustle and bustle, and the respectful silence when the actors were rehearsing or performing, they all filled me with that same sense of safety I had felt at the theater as a teenager. I was home.

€ € €

A shoot began to emerge from the seed that had been planted in my mind during my six-month stint in San Diego as an exchange student, and with it came a deep urge to travel, to go beyond the world I knew, to learn more and possibly go to college in the United States. My gut was telling me that there was something bigger out there worth exploring, a place where my outspoken nature and strong opinions wouldn't be threatened by death. By my senior year, I had landed at the top of my school's list of undesirable students. Some of my close friends made the list too. This meant the school faculty had their eyes fixed on us; they knew we were activists, although they couldn't quite prove it, so they'd come down on us hard with demerits and suspensions for everything from having our socks scrunched down around our ankles to wearing the wrong color ribbon in our hair. But they couldn't take it much further than that because, much to their chagrin, we were good students. We were lucky.

After being rattled by an economy in a downward spiral, a disastrous attempt to gain rulership of the Falkland Islands, and rising outcries about the human rights violations that were becoming increasingly evident after close to eight seemingly endless years, the military junta at long last held democratic elections, and on October 30, 1983, the people chose Raúl Alfonsín to be Argentina's next president, the man who would lead us back into a democracy. When he assumed power on December 10, celebrations echoed through the entire country and we all let out a collective sigh of relief. But in reality, no one knew if the fragile peace would hold. The fear and pain of the past eight years were still all too present within the fabric of society. We couldn't help but think: *Will this democratic government last, or is it just for show to get the human rights organizations off their back? What if I express myself a little too openly and then the military regains power? Will we have to go back to the depths of not being able to think, feel, or express ourselves freely?* People were genuinely afraid of openly speaking about that period in their lives and what they had seen or suffered. It took a couple of years for everyone to realize democracy was here to stay. So, when I was presented with the chance to leave the country right after my high school graduation as Alfonsín was taking power at the end of 1983, I didn't think twice, and I jumped at the opportunity.

I had recently ended a relationship that had left my heart shattered, and I was determined to never suffer like that again—teenage heartbreak is the worst—but when an American exchange student named Jeff came along with his good looks, charm, eloquence, and incredibly fast mind, we immediately clicked. He was visiting Rodolfo, an exchange student at his school in the United States with whom he had become close friends. Ours was a mind-melding relationship; he nourished my curiosity and consistent desire to learn more about everything and anything. We could talk for hours and feel like only minutes had passed. As I got to know him more over the next couple of months of his visit, I slowly allowed myself to let my guard down and connect with this wonderful person.

During one of our last conversation-filled dates, before he was due to return home, he suddenly looked straight into my eyes and said, "Do you want to come with me?" A huge smile spread across my face, and while my heart did backflips and somersaults, I nodded yes. This wasn't just a chance to be closer to my boyfriend; it was also a fantastic opportunity to take a gap year and spend some more time in the United States improving my English. When I told my mom, she looked at me suspiciously and said, "You're not pregnant, are you?" Once I reassured her that I wasn't, she gave me the green light to leave home.

After spending a year in Seattle with my boyfriend and realizing that I wanted to stay on and go to college there, I returned to La Plata and hit my mom with this decision and another piece of news: "I'm getting married."

My mom stood there for a second, staring at her barely nineteen-year-old daughter in disbelief, and once again asked, "Wait, are you pregnant now?"

"No, Mamá, I'm not pregnant. I love Jeff. I want to marry him. And I want to live in the States."

"Okay," she said, reluctantly.

A few days before I was due to leave again, I glanced around my room and thought, *Okay, what can I do without?* I carefully chose the items that would make me feel less alone while away from the only home I knew and packed up my life in two suitcases. That was the easy part. The hard part was having to say goodbye to my loved ones. My high school friends came over one last time, and as we sat on the floor gabbing away, a pang of melancholy gripped my heart. *Now this I will miss,* I thought. I looked at each of my buddies as they chatted, joked around, and laughed, and I was so grateful for belonging to such a loving group of humans. I knew staying in touch would be difficult. We didn't have email or WhatsApp or FaceTime in the 1980s, and long-distance calls cost an arm and a leg. When we did manage to call each other, the connections were riddled with static and echoes, so the words exchanged were succinct: "How are you . . . you . . . you?" "I'm fine." "Good, okay, you better hang up before you run up the bill." "I love you! I miss you . . . you . . . you!" *Click. Dial tone.* No room for deep talks. No room for inside jokes. Those were left for our letters, which could take a couple of weeks to reach the other person. So I soaked in the presence of my friends and only hoped I could find a similar group of people in Seattle. Material things come and go, but people are irreplaceable.

On the day of my departure, my mom and sister drove me to Ezeiza International Airport. After checking my bags at the airline's counter, we walked to the security checkpoint and joined the rest of the families who were saying their own tearful good-byes. I hugged my sister, then embraced my mother, and quietly began to cry as I walked by the guard. That day, I said goodbye to my family, my childhood, and embarked on a new adventure into the unknown, into the dawn of my adult years, ready to face my weaknesses and turn them into strengths.

❮ ❮ ❮

Going back to the MCU heroes, I can't help but think about Tony Stark's apparent weakness in *Iron Man 3*. He is suffering from PTSD after his near-death experience at the end of the Battle of New York, and the anxiety that comes with this disorder together with the thought of living in such a dangerous world compels him to make dozens of powered suits in a desperate attempt to maintain control and keep his loved ones safe. Yet that small army of suits is unable to stop his home from being attacked and destroyed. What's more, he is left stranded in a rural town in Tennessee with experimental armor that doesn't even have enough power to fly him home to California. Thrown back into a suitless world, where his weaknesses are on full display, he has to pause and rethink his way forward. And this paves a new road before him, one where his ingenuity and instincts once again have free rein. "My armor ... was never a distraction or a hobby," says Stark, by the end of his journey in *Iron Man 3*, "but a cocoon. And now, I'm a changed man." He is forced to trust himself over his armor and run toward his problems, and he doesn't just kick ass—he becomes a better human being.

Many of the situations that take place in the MCU movies

reflect what is happening in our own lives. We don't shy away from our weaknesses, because we believe there is no shame in them. Whether you go fast or slow, whether you hold the banner in the first row or fall back to the third or fourth row, whether you have panic attacks or simply feel insecure, your fighting potential is still intact. Sometimes we must retreat, reflect, and regroup in order to come back with renewed strength to fight another day and stay alive in the game. And that is absolutely okay, because that's what heroes do. Don't let anything or anyone make you ever think otherwise.

4

Consider the Light

**"We never lose our demons, Mordo.
We only learn to live above them."**

—THE ANCIENT ONE, *DOCTOR STRANGE* (2016)

We all struggle to choose between light and darkness at different points in our lives. How we view the world will determine how we experience it, and what we do with the possibilities presented along our journey is up to us. We can choose to see chaos as an insurmountable obstacle or identify the potential that lies before us. We can choose to let darkness swallow us whole, or we can choose to fight our way to the light. Think about Erik Killmonger in *Black Panther*. Brilliantly played by Michael B. Jordan, Killmonger is a villain who is convinced that he is fighting for what's right, for what will ultimately benefit the world on a larger scale. His initial hope to free the oppressed was a noble cause. Yet his drive came from a place of such profound darkness and rage that it tarnished his original intention and turned everything he touched into destruction.

At some point in his path, he was presented with a choice, with possibilities, with the opportunity to take a different road, with the chance to consider light over darkness. But he let his unabashed fury and lust for revenge obscure his journey, and his ruthless desire for power and vengeance led the way. The death of the people we love is one of the roughest cards we are dealt. The death of Erik's father turned him into someone determined to make others pay for what was done to him. He had the possibility to restore a fractured situation, but he chose violence instead. Darkness over light. In this big world of possibilities, some people choose that path because it feels like a quick solution, to take matters into their own hands. But it's a quick fix with lifelong consequences. The Mothers of the Plaza de Mayo lost their children to violence too, but time and again they chose light over darkness. They walked with love in their hearts every Thursday at the Plaza de Mayo for forty years, hoping that they would find out where their children were. They waited. Only time would reveal to some their children's whereabouts. Others never found out.

❮ ❮ ❮

Nothing in my life ever happened or arrived when I wanted it. Even my tears took their sweet time. Eight years, to be exact. Eight years of pent-up sadness. Eight years to finally release the sorrow and mourn the loss of my father. Falling in love for the first time at fifteen was my catalyst. That emotion opened the dam in my heart and allowed me to be vulnerable with my boyfriend, to let the tears flow. We will likely cry over such losses for the rest of our lives. They're part of a structure in our lives that has been abruptly torn down, suddenly leaving us with nothing. That's where choice comes into play. We can either take shelter in that pitch-black crater and fester in the shadows, replaying the wrongdoings we have had to suffer and letting our pain, humiliation, and frustration feed our rage, or we can learn to release that pain and loss, build a new structure, and set our sights on the light beyond the crater. It is not easy. But it's possible.

Erik Killmonger chose darkness. But what if he had considered the possibility of light? What if he had stepped back and taken the time to consider another option? One that let others in, one where he could ask questions, collaborate with others, and bring his concerns to light without having to leave a trail of death and destruction in his wake? As our mischievous Loki once said, "No one bad is ever truly bad. And no one good is ever truly good." This statement couldn't be truer. We are always a hair away from becoming villains ourselves, as we all must battle thoughts and feelings cloaked in darkness at some point in our lives. That's why, even though we know what they're doing is unacceptable, there's a side of us that understands villains and can even empathize with their backstories, with that moment, that choice, when it all went terribly wrong. From that place of empathy, we forge a path to compassion and forgiveness. That's why Erik Killmonger's choice of death over imprisonment is riddled with mixed emotions for the viewers and ultimately even moves T'Challa, played by the late Chadwick Boseman, to open Wakanda's borders to the world so that his cousin's demise is not in vain.

Life is far from perfect. It will never be consistently solid, joyful, or gracious, but just like our planet, it's the only one we have, and it's up to us to choose what we do with our own obstacles and periods of darkness. There are people who, much like Loki, command attention by creating chaos. I call them takers because they're on a one-way trip to drain the energy from anyone by their side. Others thrive on inciting fear or doubt by sounding the alarm on invisible dangers that likely don't even exist. The problem is that if you live in a constant state of doubt or turmoil, if you have a negative outlook on life, you will likely begin to weave your own self-fulfilling prophecy of darkness and disbelief. Because darkness attracts more darkness and only creates a larger void in your journey.

When you attempt to climb out of one of these enormous, obscure craters, you will be blinded by the light at first, but don't cower away from that source of positive energy. Grab a pair of sunglasses until you adjust to the gleam of hope and ease yourself into a new perspective. That's what I did when I set foot on the University of Washington's sprawling seven-hundred-acre campus as an undergraduate student. Talk about a gleaming light. As I stood by Drumheller Fountain (also known as Frosh Pond for its hundred-year association with pranks pulled on first-year students) in the heart of the majestic Rainier Vista walkway, surrounded by collegiate Gothic buildings and a medley of trees framing the magnificent snowcapped Cascade Range in the distance, I thought, *I can't believe I'm here. I can't believe this is my school and I will be learning from these minds.*

I was finally in a place where I could express myself freely without fear of repercussions and was overwhelmed with gratitude for such an amazing opportunity, even if I still lacked the ability to fully communicate who I was in English. But reading and writing weren't a problem, so I felt confident I had this second language in the bag—until I arrived at my layover in LAX on my way to Seattle and a man spoke to me so fast I couldn't make out a word he said. A quiet panic set in. *Oh my goodness, what have I done? I don't know what he's saying. Was moving here even the right choice?* After blankly staring back at the man, not knowing how to respond, I shook these doubts out of my mind and said to myself, *Well, I better start understanding, because this is my life now.* I repeated to him what I thought he was saying, and, after a few verbal bumps and a couple of laughs, my bags were taken care of. I had summited the first small hill of many to come.

It was not easy. But it was possible.

❮ ❮ ❮

At the beginning, I struggled. All my energy was primarily focused on surviving the day-to-day in my new home. So much of who we are is hampered when our verbal communication is limited; it's almost as if we become a lightly sketched silhouette of ourselves. And for someone like me, with an endless curiosity and an overactive mind, who thrives on social interactions and the exchange of ideas, it felt quite isolating. I depended solely on other people's patience in conversation—sometimes it was seamless, and other times it took an extra minute for me to harness and translate my more complex thoughts and then express them in a way that communicated my passions, interests, and philosophies to the person quietly waiting for me to form my sentences. This quickly taught me who was genuinely keen on getting to know me and whose interest suddenly dissolved when I couldn't find the right words in the expected time frame.

Not one to give up, I pressed on, determined to bring my conversation skills up to par. I couldn't add another course to my fully loaded semester and didn't have time to sit on the campus grass leisurely hanging out with new friends—I was a full-time student, a newlywed, and a server working nightshifts at Azteca, a nearby restaurant. I needed to find something that would teach me everyday expressions, colloquialisms, and social cues during the free windows I had between classes: Enter soap operas *Days of Our Lives*, *As the World Turns*, and *Santa Barbara* featuring A Martinez, the American soap world's very first Latin lead.

Yes, soap operas, that's what I turned to. They taught me everything I needed to know about how Americans express themselves and why a certain inflection in an "All's well" answer to the question "How are you?" might be code for being nice but not wanting to engage in further conversation. Better still, these soaps stretched out the same issue throughout an entire week. On Mondays, the issue was revealed. On Tuesdays, the main characters shared the issue with their friends or families. On Wednesdays, the villains found out about the issue and sought to make it even worse. On Thursdays, the main characters enlisted the help of their loved ones to fight the issue together, and by Fridays, the issue was usually resolved, and we were left on a cliff-hanger that opened the door to a whole other issue the following week. This slow burn exposed me to repetition and the discussion of one topic from different points of view. I might not have quite grasped the gist of the issue on Monday, but by Friday I totally understood that the husband had murdered his wife and while he tried to hide the evidence, the others were desperately trying to bring it to light. Along the way, if I didn't understand a particular word, I'd quickly look it up in my dictionary and repeat it a few times to cement it in my growing vocabulary. Within a few months, I was finally able to find my stride and break the language barrier that had been holding me back since my arrival. Now all I had to do was find a gang of friends to mimic what I used to have with my own group back in La Plata. That would prove harder to accomplish.

Seattle is a wonderful city, bursting at the seams with deep-green trees, stunning mountains, tranquil lakes, and islands dotting the Puget Sound. You can ski *and* play tennis, weather permitting. I even learned to live with the rain and not let it stop me from going out for a jog or enjoying the outdoors, but I was still far removed from almost everyone I loved. I missed my mom. I missed my friends. I missed our talks. Fortunately, I had Jeff. He was my light in that transition. We were great partners, and he was also one of my closest friends. Since we both went to UW and had similar schedules, we'd drive to campus together. Then we'd spend the evenings together working at Azteca in Federal Way. When he was transferred to another location in the evenings, I became closer to a fellow server, Kathy, the best friend I could've asked for. She's American but also speaks Spanish, so whenever I got stuck midsentence with a customer, she'd bail me out. Oftentimes, at the end of our shift, we'd break into guacamole fights, giggle like kids, and then drive over to the local twenty-four-hour grocery store to do our shopping before heading back home. With Jeff and now Kathy, life became less lonely, and I settled into my routine.

During the next four years, I went to college from eight a.m. to around three p.m., rushed home, changed into my work clothes, and began my four p.m. to eleven p.m. serving shift at Azteca—a job I needed, since my financial aid only covered the bare minimum at school. Once my shift was over, I headed back home with Jeff, hit the books while I rubbed my sore feet, then went to sleep and repeated my routine all over again the next day. As if that weren't enough, at the start of each semester I chose to seek the light by showing up to the classes I wanted to take, even if they had been deemed full. The professors always approached me by the end of the hour and whispered, "You know this class is closed, right?"

"Yeah, I know," I replied confidently, and continued to show up diligently every week.

I knew that at some point someone would usually end up dropping out of class, and when that happened, I wanted to be ready and waiting to pounce on that spot without missing a beat. I also knew I had to be present from the start to officially join the class, if and when there was an unexpected opening. So I made it a priority to be there.

The idea that something doesn't have to be taken at face value, that we can make it what we need, has always been a part of who I am, my essence. As Kamala Khan says in *Ms. Marvel*, "There is no normal. There's just us and what we do with what we've been given." Sure, those classes I showed up for were full and closed to new students. Sure, chances were I was wasting my time. But I just figured if by the end of the first few weeks no one had dropped out and I was unable to get into the course, I would at least have the upper hand when I took it the following semester because the content would be familiar and easier to digest. Every class I was wait-listed for had a student drop out, and I gleefully took their spot. Many professors told me they had never seen someone so determined to beat the system and find a different way. There's the nucleus of our circumstances (class is full), and then there's the periphery (the possibility of a dropout). I've always looked outside the box; that's why I tend to find most of my answers on the periphery. Limitations, hurdles, challenges, whatever you want to call them, they're there to push us to new heights and allow us to consider the light at the top of the mountain.

When the time came to declare my career path, I chose to double major in theater and psychology. That's when I began to delve deeper into what it means to animate a written piece and bring it to a live audience. I got my feet wet with *Animal Farm*. Cast as the lead hen, I didn't have too many lines, so I was able to quietly observe the comings and goings not just of the actors but also of the backstage crew, pitching in where I could and learning the ropes along the way. Doing so led me to further discover the vast layers of the theater's production department—a different scale from the high school play and La Lechuza experiences; it was mesmerizing to be a part of it. The illusions that could be created through ingenious lighting, sound, and the well-choreographed dance that happens backstage to bring a work to life on the main stage all captured my attention and curiosity. And in that moment, unbeknownst to me, another seed was planted. One that would take a few years to sprout, but it would do so when I was good and ready to aim for those purported glass ceilings.

❝ ❝ ❝

When people wonder what obstacles I've confronted in my path, I think they are usually looking for a very solid mountain, but I see that mountain as the sum of the many smaller stones and pebbles we all must encounter along our journeys. No path is satin smooth. Setting aside life-altering events, which are the craters we've been talking about, everyday life can be seen as an obstacle course. Getting out of the house when your kid refuses to wear a jacket on a cold day is an obstacle. Traffic is an obstacle. Inclement weather is an obstacle. Our boss asking us to redo a task we thought we'd done well in the first place is an obstacle. Getting tongue-tied at a meeting is an obstacle. Disagreeing with your partner is an obstacle. On most days, we are likely to confront at least one of these stones on our path. But what do we choose to do with these impediments? Do we let them taint our entire day, or can we swerve around them and instead focus on what's important in that moment? Do we choose to seek light, or bury ourselves in the darkness?

Consider this: Of the 1,000 ideas I came up with in a day at

Marvel, 998 would get rejected and only 2 would become part of the conversation at work. Then one could get cut out of the film or TV show due to length, while the other one would actually *make the cut!* When the day was over, I didn't leave work focused on the 999 ideas that were discarded. Even though my batting average might have seemingly sucked, I left that space focused on the one idea that was chosen. I got up every morning with that one idea in mind, and it inspired me to bring another 1,000 ideas to the table the next day because I knew that even though the other 999 were rejected, they helped take the conversation in new directions. I know it's easier said than done. But that's one of my secrets. That's what I mean when I talk about living in the light. It's not easy, but it's possible.

❝ ❝ ❝

My best friend, Alejo, gets a kick out of saying I live five seconds ahead of time. Not many people can see beyond the now and into tomorrow and activate, but that's also my way of living in the light—living in the joy of tomorrow's possibility rather than clinging to the pain of yesterday's hardship. And it's what I aim to do for the stories on-screen too. Sometimes, all we need in order to change how we view the world and attract more light into our lives is to see more people who look like us in positions that inspire us to aim for more, to do more, to be more.

For so many decades, we've lived in a world where scores of children around the world grew up without ever seeing themselves reflected on the big screen, in magazines, on TV, and so forth. If no one like you has superpowers or can wear a cape or save the world or be president or a model or an actor or a reporter, it's likely there will be a voice in your head that wonders, *What's wrong with me? Why aren't there more people like me out there?* Thankfully that is changing now. Because, like the Geena Davis Institute says, "If they can see it, they can be it." It's a reaffirmation that you're good just as you are—your beauty lies in your uniqueness.

Being a part of that shift in the film industry has been thrilling. To be able to represent a wide variety of people—gay, straight, Black, brown, white, rich, poor, thin, curvy, Deaf, blind, short, tall—in the Marvel films and shows allowed us to tell the world there is nothing less about a person if they don't fit the "standard mold." We all harbor a host of abilities unique to us that will allow us to win the day. To have the chance to show this in superhero form was like having a great dessert and adding a spoonful of dulce de leche on top.

This is our dulce de leche moment, a chance to give visibility to those who have always felt invisible, to show that a world of possibility exists for all of us regardless of our circumstances. And that world isn't just on the big screen—it's within you. Films are, in part, a conduit to help us get this message to you. Oftentimes, when someone sees themselves reflected in a story, it can serve as the catalyst they need to shift their perspective and begin to see glimpses of light in whatever darkness they're facing. The ultimate goal is not only having characters who show us the span of human emotions but also having every child represented.

There was a default belief in the film industry that stories like

Black Panther and *Captain Marvel* would never work, that they would be a fiscal debacle because a Black cast and a female super-hero would not be box office hits on opening weekend. The issue was that the stats we needed to back our budgets and get them approved under what would be considered fiscally responsible levels just didn't exist. Therefore, on paper, they were not good ideas, but in our guts, we knew they were. So we charged ahead toward the light. Rather than focus on the barriers we kept banging into, we decided to set our eyes on making the best movies possible and letting them speak for themselves.

Sounds like a risky move, right? You bet it was. But that's the nature of the movie business—you never truly know if it will be a good movie or a great success unless you make it. Those two movies didn't just go on to earn more than $2 billion; they also helped us create the stats to prove that future stories like these two are worth telling.

When people see *Black Panther* or *Captain Marvel* now, they probably think they're no-brainers, but they have no idea the hurdles we faced to get them off the ground. I'm happy they became box office hits, but if they hadn't, they would've still provided a valuable lesson: We need to take risks regardless of whether they will pay off in the end. Taking risks pushes us to forge a space for our dreams and pave the way to make them a reality. And failure is not darkness, nor a crater or a hurdle or an obstacle; it's a lesson in growth. My view of the world and the choices I made paved the way to my burgeoning career. I don't think I would've made it this far if I had remained wallowing in the craters I had to face early on. So take the hit, deal with it, get back up, and keep moving toward the light. Consider taking action when you fall. Consider a lighter moment when your outlook feels dark. Consider the possibilities before you. The choice is yours. You have the power to live above your demons, because you are light. And light attracts light.

5

Why Not?

"All we can do is our best, and sometimes
the best that we can do is to start over."

—PEGGY CARTER, *CAPTAIN AMERICA: THE WINTER SOLDIER* (2014)

How different would your life be if you truly and honestly considered your options and learned to live in a heightened state of possibility?

If I hadn't considered applying for an exchange program that took me to San Diego to further my English skills, I wouldn't have been exposed to another way of life. If I hadn't considered marrying a man who lived in Seattle, I wouldn't have gone to college there. If I hadn't considered talking to a friend of a friend about working in production, I wouldn't have embarked on a career of thirty-plus years that led me to be president of physical and postproduction, visual effects, and animation at the studio with the highest-grossing film franchise of all time. And it all started with my mom, with her belief in me. When I was a kid, she never told me that I couldn't. Remember, she always said, "If it has been done, you can do it. But if it hasn't been done, you should." That created a big enough threshold for me to cross. From then on, no matter how small or far-fetched the idea might have seemed, I chose to consistently consider any and all possibilities and ask myself: *Hmm, what if I do that? Well, why not?*

Possibilities come in many forms. They are the chances we take; they inspire the choices we make; they are the doors we decide to open and the roads that lead us to find and shape our path. So, what is the path? Consider this question: If you could be or do anything, what would *you* choose? In everybody's life, whether we are able to openly accept it or not, there are things that we are innately attracted to. I see the path as our passion, our calling, that thing that keeps tugging at us, that continuously crosses our mind even if it seems unattainable. It's that one constant in our lives that, no matter how many doors get slammed in our face, consistently keeps our light. That path will reveal itself to be our purpose.

Sometimes our paths aren't so clearly defined from the get-go. Sometimes we may think we're following our path, only to realize halfway down the way that it was actually a path someone else envisioned for us. Say you grew up with traditional parents. They may have implicitly set you on a certain path based on their expectations of what they wanted for you—marrying someone of the opposite sex, having children by a certain age, moving away from the dangerous city to a safer house in the suburbs. If that path feels right to you, then great. But if it doesn't, if something is pulling you in a different direction, urging you to consider other possibilities, then it may be time to quiet the noise and chatter around you and honestly listen to your own voice. The choice is always yours. Just listen.

There's a constant voice that remains alive within us over time and space, no matter how many obstacles or how many events, in how ever many ways, try to kill it throughout the years. That's the path to who we are. Our purpose. The path can be your reality, or it can be something you long for and dream of but aren't necessarily following...yet. Oftentimes, people choose not to follow their real path because it may demand too much of a shake-up, too huge of an effort, without the guarantee that it's going to work out. The fear of the unknown, of not being sure if you're journeying down the right way, may stop you in your tracks. *What if I'm wrong, and what if all these people are right?*

It's hard to abandon something that you know will give you a little for something that could potentially give you so much more when that potential is not a guarantee. Ultimately, that's a conversation you can only have with yourself. But if you don't go for it, if you don't consider that possibility, if you don't listen to your voice, you risk shutting down and silencing a part of you. And by not paying attention to that part of you, little by little, you'll start chipping away at your inner light, until it eventually dims and switches off, sometimes forever.

My marriage to Jeff was solid through college—we made a great team. After he graduated, he started working at Alaska Airlines, where he had access to affordable standby tickets that allowed us to travel the world for the next couple of years. We globe-trotted across Europe, visited Jamaica, and spent quality time in Argentina with my family and friends. Flying standby required flexibility. On a few occasions we left the house thinking we were heading to Paris and ended up in Amsterdam due to an unforeseen full flight. But we just went with the flow. Traveling is an interesting relationship barometer; it brings out our anxieties, our comfort levels, who's okay winging it in another language, who's okay making reservations or following directions, and ultimately how we react when things don't go as planned. Jeff and I traveled well together but usually wanted to do different things once we arrived. He wanted to make the most of each visit by hitting the key museums and landmarks, while I wanted to sit at a café, people watch, chat, and simply process my surroundings and take it all in. Neither possibility was right or wrong—it was just different, to the point where I remember once having a fleeting thought after coming back home from one of these trips: *Will we be able to keep this up in the long run?* It's those moments of lucidity that we have in relationships or in our careers that we bury away as silly thoughts and years later wonder why we didn't pay more attention to them.

With time, the small cracks in our marriage turned into a crater that was impossible to ignore. He was a good friend, but I think toward the end of our relationship our disparity became stronger than our connection. There were painful moments, irreconcilable differences, and, after several years, my graduation, and two moves—first to San Francisco and then to Los Angeles—the time came to call it quits and forge a new path. Suddenly, I went from a married twentysomething to being on my own for the first time in my adulthood. I had to search for a roommate and get another job in a relatively new city to make ends meet. Yet, although it was a painful transition, I didn't let it obscure the possibilities I now had within my reach.

One of my favorite lines from *Avengers: Endgame* is between Thor and his mother, Frigga. Thor has gone back in time to see his mother, and she's worried because he doesn't appear to be well—he has gained a lot of weight, let himself go, and seems to have thrown in the towel. Noticing how sad and depressed he is, Frigga says, "Everyone fails at who they're supposed to be, Thor. The measure of a person, of a hero, is how well they succeed at being who they are." These words have resonated deeply within me and stayed incredibly present since I read them in the script. It is so wise of Frigga to point out that the only success her son should worry about is being the best self he can be. Not someone else's self or the idea of self. His very own self. The road to discover that self is grounded in the purpose that consistently fills our free time and finds a way to stick around even when we ignore it. Tune in to that feeling to find your best self. Choose the path that makes you feel whole. Don't let others define your future based on the possibilities *they* see for you. By doing that, you are limiting those possibilities to what they believe you are supposed to be rather than opening up to your own hopes and dreams to allow you to be you. When faced with the possibility of creating your own path, as scary as it may seem to go it alone, it's worth considering and giving it a shot because you never know where it may lead.

I was convinced that if I wanted to be a storyteller, I had to be an actor. That's what I grew up doing in the theater years earlier in Argentina, then at college in Seattle, so I just took it as a given. As I settled into the rhythm of my new hometown of Los Angeles, one thing was clear: I had to set my life up to survive and also allow for the weekly grind of auditions. That is, I had to explore different avenues that would keep me heading down my path. I was in the process of getting divorced. I didn't have a lot of money and I refused to ask my mother for any help, so I got a job at Alaska Airlines as an agent. They immediately saw my bilingualism as an asset and put me in charge of international departures and arrivals, since they had several flights to and from Mexico. Another bonus: This job provided me with health insurance. But what I loved the most was that I could eat the leftover first-class food, which took care of at least one of my meals while I was on shift.

Then I got another job as a server at Black Angus on the weekends. I loved being a server and was told I was great at it. I already had five years of experience working through college at the Azteca Mexican restaurant in the Seattle area. Back then, I knew the families, I knew the kids; there were some regulars who came at least once a week. I watched them laugh and fight, I witnessed them fall in love, and I saw how they taught their children to be careful not to burn their mouths eating the hot beans. These people were part of my work family, and every one of those details filled me with warmth. My Black Angus experience wasn't as intimate because I spent less than a year there, with far fewer shifts—but I did get to eat steak every weekend.

Getting a foot into the studios in Los Angeles with no

connections can feel daunting, but I was determined to find a way. I was looking for my one shot, the side door that would let me come in and prove that I had what it took, even though I didn't have the credentials or experience. Before or after my work shifts, I would drive to the studios, park my car, and walk in like I knew where I was going. When a guard approached me, I'd quickly glance at their name tag and throw in a "Hey, John, how's it going?" as if we'd seen each other yesterday. They'd reply with a disconcerted "Hi . . ." visibly trying to place me, and I'd just wave and keep on walking. The next week, I'd walk by and say, "Hey, John!" and get a smile and a "Hey, how's it going?" in response. By the third week, the guard knew my name. One time, one of the guards stopped me and asked, "So, where do you work?" And I replied honestly in a whisper, "I'm actually still trying to get a job." In awe of my perseverance, he said, "Tell you what, I'm going to talk to someone on the inside."

My chitchat didn't stop at the entrance either. Once I was inside, I approached people on their coffee or smoke breaks for some small talk, they'd point me in the direction of other people, and eventually someone would say, "Hey, that department is hiring." That's how I became a page at Paramount. From the outside, no one was hiring. But by being on the inside, even just as an outsider looking in, I was ready and willing when a door eventually did open, just like I was during college as a standby student waiting for someone to drop out. Now, I'm not advocating this road for everyone. It probably wouldn't work as smoothly nowadays in this age of heightened security, but my point is that there is always a possibility if you're willing to say *Why not?* and explore it.

The possibility of not finding a job never crossed my mind. What did cross my mind was *I hope I like whatever job I get.*

I handled the tours and worked the three-camera sitcoms and late-night shows. And guess what? They fed me too—live shows usually have food for their staff. Do you see an emerging trend here? Yes, my jobs revolved around food, but I'm actually far from a hardcore foodie. This was more about survival, a means to an end. I made just enough money to cover my rent and my car, so learning how to source my meals without having to worry about that specific expense was a huge relief. If I had nothing at home, I'd fast in the morning knowing that I'd eventually be able to eat at one of my three jobs that day. This setup also meant that I didn't have to cook, which was fine by me. I can barbecue, but I'm not a huge fan of toiling away in the kitchen. So there you have it, three different roads that provided health insurance, food, and a foot in the door with a studio, which all helped me keep moving along my path.

When I think back to being a page at Paramount I'm filled with lightness—it was the early days of dreaming. Dreaming about Hollywood, about the possibilities of what could happen in my career. My fellow page and friend Jeanie King, who's now VP of production and a senior executive visual effects producer at Industrial Light & Magic (ILM), and I would take the golf cart on our breaks, drive to the parking lot, which was sometimes transformed into the Blue Sky Tank to shoot water scenes, and daydream of our plans for the future and where we'd be twenty to thirty years from then. We vowed to keep in touch regardless of where our paths took us, and sure enough, we still work together today. I'd give tours of the lot and stages and recount Paramount's glorious history as the longest-operating major studio in Hollywood and the extensive list of acting royalty who had walked through the studio's emblematic Bronson Gate, everyone from Gloria Swanson, Mary Pickford, Rudolph Valentino, and Douglas Fairbanks to Bing Crosby, Marlene Dietrich, John Wayne, and Elvis Presley. But my favorite story was that of the fountain just beyond that gate. To this day, I'm not sure if it's a true story or not, but legend has it that the fountain was added across from the two-story buildings that flanked the gate to muffle the private conversations seeping through the open windows on hot summer days (that is, until the air conditioner became more mainstream).

When I saw famous people walking by I learned to play it cool, as it was part of my job, until the day I was slowly driving down one of the studio's back lots and someone said, "Hi, do you know how to get to the ADR stage?" That's the automated dialogue replacement stage, the studio where many actors go to rerecord certain parts of a film's audio in a quieter setting to improve the sound quality of their dialogue. I looked up, and when I noticed the person standing behind the man speaking to me, I thought, *Oh my God, oh my God, it's Robert De Niro!* My heart raced. His movie credits scrolled through my mind: *Taxi Driver, Raging Bull, The Untouchables, Goodfellas, Awakenings.* Ahhh! Starstruck to the max, I simply answered, "Yes, yes, I do." And that was it. I didn't give them directions to the ADR stage, not even a hint of how to get there. I just went silent. The guy looked back at me, slightly puzzled. "Okay, so where is it?" And with that, I snapped back to reality and quickly replied, "Oh, hop on, I'll take you." So there I was, with Robert De Niro in the back seat of my golf cart, and all I could think was: *What an idiot! I just got totally tongue-tied with Mr. De Niro.* He was very sweet and gracious, as was his team, and when we arrived at their destination I said, "I'm so sorry, I just didn't know what to say when I saw you." They smiled knowingly. "It's okay, you got a little shy," said one of the guys with Mr. De Niro. I smiled back as they waved and walked away.

❮ ❮ ❮

Throughout the years, I have stayed on my path, but, as you have seen, my roads along the way have varied. Sometimes they've been bumpy; occasionally they've been a little smoother. Whether it's a dirt road or a cobblestone street or freshly poured concrete, I will walk on anything to follow my path (except, maybe, nails . . . You know, everyone has their limit). Please consider these different roads when you come across them. Sometimes they may be shorter and more direct; other times you may meander down a few side streets that delay your journey but teach you a valuable lesson; and sometimes you may choose an alley or dead end that simply exposes you to beautiful scenery, filling you with inspiration and allowing you to reenter your path feeling lighter and freer than before. All the possibilities are exciting, so long as they don't veer too far off your main path, because they all serve one purpose: experience.

Whenever I booked an audition, I would move my shifts around to accommodate the opportunity and make it work. I got a few parts in the Bilingual Foundation of the Arts productions because they did plays in both Spanish and English, so I was a good fit there. And I worked with Grupo de Teatro SINERGIA and its artistic director, Ruben Amavizca, who I'm still in touch with today. But in the TV and film world, my highlights came down to a few walk-on parts on *The Young and the Restless, The Bold and the Beautiful*, and *Thirtysomething*. I was cast as a nanny in *The Bold and the Beautiful* and had only two lines: "Hello, Mr. Spencer" and "Mark had a wonderful day." End scene. But this was the best gig of the three. Not only did I get to say two lines, but I also got to be on set as a jury member in a court scene that took three entire weeks to film—God bless intrigue and soaps for repeating the story the whole week long!

Life and its possibilities work in mysterious ways: The soaps that had taught me conversational English and social cues seven years earlier were now the few that booked me for some tiny roles. But they were scarce—I got many more noes than yeses. Nevertheless, every night, I'd sit down in my apartment's small living room, and, rather than focus on the day's rejections, I'd zero in on the lessons. There were times when I didn't learn much about the audition process itself, but I did learn a whole lot about myself. I'd think of the different roads I could take next, hoping one would lead to a positive outcome. Obviously, I knew rejection was part of the acting game, but a couple of years later, it really started to take a toll on me. After endless auditions, I realized I kept getting the same feedback:

"You're too tall."

"You're too short."

"You're too fat."

"You're too slim."

"You have an accent."

"You don't have an accent."

"You don't look Latin, are you Latin?"

"You're too white."

I never cared about the roads I had to take to follow my path, but I also began to understand that there was only so much of this rejection I was willing to go through. This was not for me. I have a lot of respect for actors because it takes a very thick skin to put up with the invariable rejection that comes with that craft. And I have pretty thick skin, but not landing a role would upset me, and then knowing in my heart that I was unsettled by something that wasn't really the path for me would upset me even more. I'm sure casting directors and producers could see that too. I could take some logical turndowns, but when it comes to getting rejected as an actor, most of the time you don't know the reasons why you don't get the parts. And that didn't fit my personality. I couldn't live my life on hold, at the mercy of someone else's criteria. I didn't want my destiny to be in the hands of others at that level. Having someone else decide my future is just not in my makeup. Some people can wait for the "You got the role!" phone call—and, believe me, we love those people, we need our actors. But all I wanted to do each time I didn't get that call was go to that production office to figure out why, and talk things over to see if we could fix it or if I could learn from that moment so as not to repeat the same mistake. I was an innate producer, and I didn't even know it!

No is a limitation of something. When I consider a *no*, to this day, I'm always interested in the *why* behind it. So much so that when someone on my team says, "No, we can't shoot that,"

I always dig deeper into that limitation—is it a money issue, a time issue, a weather issue, or some other hurdle?—and see if we can fill that gap, turn that no around, and make what someone declares impossible actually possible. We confronted these types of limitations on a small and large scale daily on just about every set, and we did our best to surpass them when possible. Take, for example, Marvel's TV series *Loki*. When we started filming, Sophia Di Martino, the female Loki, had a newborn at home and was breastfeeding, which meant that she needed to take breaks to pump for her baby. But the suit made the whole process incredibly uncomfortable, so she came to us and explained the situation. The costumes had already been made, but we talked to our costume designer, Christine Wada, and she got to work and customized Sophia's outfit by adding concealed zippers for easy access when she needed to pump. This is a small yet great example of teamwork, the result of having more women on set to understand such a situation, and what happens when you consider other possibilities. At the end of the day, when your actors are more comfortable performing, it will make for a better scene, so it was a win-win all around.

Another no that we turned into a yes at Marvel was when we were tasked to shoot additional photography at the end of *Thor: The Dark World*. We were faced with a conundrum because the director, Alan Taylor, had to remain in Los Angeles to finish the movie, and we had Natalie Portman and Chris Hemsworth in two different parts of the world. It would've been impossible to get them all in the same place, so we had to figure out a way around this limitation. We put technology to work here and decided to shoot Chris with a double, who happened to be his wife, for the final postcredits kiss scene, and then we composited the shot. We could've just run with a *no* and not had that now viral scene, but instead we considered the possibilities and made it happen.

Nevertheless, in different productions, when all options were explored and we concluded none of them made sense, oftentimes I was the one who said no. But I surrounded myself with a team that, like me, wouldn't take no for an answer without a fight for the possibility of a yes. For example, one time, my team asked if we could finish the color timing of our TV projects in-house instead of hiring an outside vendor, and after considering it, I said no. I explained that I thought it would entail managing an even bigger group of people and would take up a lot of their time—time we didn't have to spare. Plus, we had been working pretty seamlessly with the vendors, so it didn't make sense to me. But they pushed for their idea: "Just let us show you how we could do it." I conceded and, contrary to what I had concluded, bringing these tasks in-house made the process more time efficient and less expensive because it cut down on the hours we spent sending and receiving files externally. So I turned to them and said, "You were absolutely right, thank you for insisting on showing me this possibility." It's not about who's right or who's wrong; that's not the storyteller's way—that's the way of an egomaniac. I don't need to be right. I need to support whatever plan helps make our movies better.

Of course, sometimes, there's just no way around a no, and that has to be okay—as long as you've taken the time to consider all the possibilities beforehand. The key is to stay open and willing to listen, because there may be a point in the *why* of that no, and it is something worth considering when making future decisions. Or simply to grow. I think it's safe to say I have received more from every no that I have gotten than from some of the yeses, because those noes taught me something or inspired me to take another path that led to an unimaginable outcome. So it is true, I live in the world of possibility, but I also understand that sometimes what we expect won't work. And that's when we have to learn to let go. The key to not getting stuck is to know *when* to let go. The power of *no* led me to a road of resilience. A road I have traveled extensively on my path to success. Sometimes encountering a *no* will lead to a necessary door in the path to your own purpose.

❝ ❝ ❝

One day, during those early years auditioning in Los Angeles, after going through the rejection mill one too many times, I finally asked, "Who makes the decisions?"

"The producers," said the casting director.

Then that's what I'm going to be, I said to myself. I let go. Being stuck doesn't suit me.

The truth is, I'm a terrible actor. I can't learn someone else's words, because I always want to put my spin on them. If you give me a script, I'll start reading it, and then pause and say, "I'm not sure that's how I would say it." That should've been the first sign acting wasn't for me! Deep down, I wasn't interested in embodying someone else; I wanted to be me. I had pursued acting because it was what I knew—the stage represented safety, but it just didn't come naturally to me. A real actor, and a good one at that, knows how to become one with the words they're given so as to become the character they're playing. Meanwhile, I wanted to edit the writer's hard work to fit me.

Up until then, I didn't quite understand that being a part of this entertainment world, being a storyteller, didn't mean only having to stand in front of the camera. When I realized that I could stay true to my path *behind* the camera too, that was it. I got there by sort of meandering through what life threw at me, but all those roads added up to that moment, that shift in goals, that course correction, and I never looked back. I will be forever grateful for that slew of rejections and those failed auditions because they made me question my current road and then find a different one that would still allow me to stay on my path.

As each of these pieces of the puzzle started to come together, I talked to my friend Alison at Alaska Airlines one day about the pivot I was considering into production, and she said, "I think you'd be great at production. Hey, you should talk to my friend Carla." Carla was a first assistant director who could give me insight on the production side of TV and films, which I knew nothing about. "Yeah, I'd love to chat with your friend," I replied without hesitation. And in that moment, something clicked.

Part of the reason for the gift of where I am today is because I never closed the door to possibility, not once. Not even now. I'm consistently open-minded and say: "Sure, I'll do that." "What? Okay, I'll do that too." You never know what door that yes is going to open. For someone like me who thrives on curiosity and gets bored pretty easily, learning is exactly what I need in my life. Considering the possibility and saying yes to meeting Alison's friend Carla paved the way for an unexpected turn in my professional path.

"There's a production assistant gig coming up. Alison said you might be interested," Carla told me when we spoke.

"Yes, I'll give it a go, but I don't know anything about production. I've never done it before."

"Don't worry," she replied. "I'll teach you."

In that moment, I decided to leave acting behind and start pursuing the decision-making producer role. In a way, it was a role I had been embodying since my dad passed away and I started filling the gaps in my family life: It even trickled down into how I behaved at school and with my friends. I just naturally hopped in and helped produce a gathering, an event, a party. My home was the meeting spot for whatever my friends and I were up to on the weekends or school holidays. I coordinated and produced student gatherings, I produced my study abroad opportunity, and I produced my move to the United States. Part of seeking a career that gave me more control over decisions was to heal the emotional scar of the loss of my father. I couldn't control that life-altering event in my life, but I could control other areas. Eventually the journey became something beyond filling that loss; it became a fulfilling career. It's been over thirty years, and I have loved every day since.

The beauty of life is in the curves, all the meandering, the diverse roads that lead you down your path. And those curves are everything. When I'm asked why I did something, or how I got to where I am today, I usually say, "Because I considered it—I considered the possibility."

❦ ❦ ❦

The roads of possibilities down to our path lead to doors that open to unforeseen journeys in our lives. In our movie *Doctor Strange*, Benedict Cumberbatch plays renowned surgeon Stephen Strange, who, after the accident that injures his hands, effectively ending his career, sets on a quest to heal himself, which leads him to Kamar-Taj, a Tibetan city hidden deep in the Himalayas. Despite his scientific mind and arrogance, he considers the possibility of seeking out the Ancient One and has to knock on an actual door to enter the compound. By taking that chance, by considering a possibility that didn't really fit his schematic and crossing that threshold, he discovers an entirely new road map that will allow him to continue on his path to help humankind with his hands, just not how he'd envisioned it. He doesn't arrive at this door immediately. It takes him months of trial and error, pain, and lashing out, but he considers each possibility and opens each one of those doors along the way until he finds the one that leads him back to his purpose. If Dr. Strange didn't seek out alternative ways to heal his hands, he wouldn't have discovered that special door that opens him up to another dimension in his path and gives him a reason to live.

Every door is the beginning of something. Open it, see where it takes you, and don't fret too much if it doesn't work out. Part of living in possibility is knowing that there will be doors that will be shut. But they shouldn't define your next move. Don't get stuck at the doorknob that just won't budge. If you are sure there is a path for you there but you can't get in through the main door, find another way in through a side door, a window, or a skylight, because that next door may hold what you've been seeking all along. Even if it's the doggy door!

Think about it: If you're at a party, no one is going to ask you, *Hey, did you come in through the front door or the garage?* because they'll usually assume you used the front entrance like everyone else. Guess what? No one cares about *how* you got there—you did it, you're in. You're at the party, you're at the meeting, you're at the table, you're in the room. What matters now is what you do once you're there. This has been an essential part of my journey.

We may not necessarily know what we're capable of doing at first, but if we know our limitations and what we are not great at, then that's where we can start. My career journey began with me first figuring out what I wasn't good at. I tried acting, but the process didn't bring me the happiness I had hoped to find. And the constant stream of rejections in a way triggered my abandonment issues, which I carried from losing my father. I couldn't keep putting little Victoria in that position any longer. It was too painful. Eventually, by slamming that door shut, I made space for me to consider opening a different one into the unknown world of production.

Life is constantly changing direction, and we have to learn how to flow with it and pay attention to how we evolve and what we may need to adjust along the way to feed our soul in the different stages of our lives. You don't have to have it all figured out. If you're not good in one position in your industry, explore other doors and see where they take you.

I opened the door to the United States, considered it, and thought, *Yeah, it would be good to live in a different country.* I opened the door to acting and eventually realized that it wasn't the road for me, so I shut it and opened a side door, the one that led to production, and there I thought, *Yeah, it would be cool to make movies.*

We are all potential, and we are filled with possibilities. That's why, if you are part of my team, I don't care to know your limitations as much as I care to know your potential. Because you may think you're limited, and I may find that you're not. I've had many people who have worked on my teams eventually say to me, "I never thought we would . . ." to which I've answered, "I always thought we could."

That's what happened at Marvel with *Black Panther*. As I mentioned earlier, the widespread belief in the industry was that no one would want to see it, that it wouldn't be a fiscal success, that the world wasn't ready for a Black superhero or, for that matter, an entirely Black cast. But we considered the possibilities and went for it anyway. In everything we did at Marvel, we weighed the risk versus the outcome, but in this case, after considering the potential outcome, the risk became unimportant. We believed this movie with Black Panther's origin story would have an impact, but we were completely blown away by the final results. Millions upon millions of people considered Wakanda, considered an African royal family, and fell in love with *Black Panther*. It fulfilled every dream of possibility, and more and more and more.

So, yes, please take what life presents you into consideration. And sometimes you just need one person believing in you to help you see the possibilities along your path. Take that into consideration too. When you tell me that I can't do something, I consider it a challenge to prove that I can. It lights a spark in me that pushes me to go get it even more. And not because I want to prove you wrong, but because I want to stretch myself into that possibility of what I can do. I take the no and I make sure to bounce right back to that heightened state of possibility.

Please, please, please consider the roads presented along your path. Consider opening all doors. Consider the possibilities. And when you question why you should, I ask you: *Why not?*

6

Jump Before You Think You're Ready

"Higher, further, faster, baby."

—CAPTAIN MARVEL, *CAPTAIN MARVEL* (2019)

What happens when you jump before you're ready? Are we ever ready? If we let our minds truly control what we do all the time, would we even get out of bed? So much of what we do is on instinct, so why don't we do more of that? What is stopping us? Why do we censor our potential before it even has a chance?

I hadn't led a studio's physical and postproduction, visual effects, and animation before I was asked to be a part of the team that ran Marvel Studios. I was clueless when it came to visual effects until I landed a job at a visual effects company. I didn't know anything about production before I set foot on a set. But when offered these possibilities, I chose to jump in headfirst and go, as Carol Danvers from *Captain Marvel* says, "higher, further, faster," regardless of how prepared or experienced I might have been for the job. Much like the seven test pilots chosen by NASA in 1959 to blast into the unknown on a rocket-fueled spacecraft to determine if humans could fly in space and come back to tell the story. Yes, they were trained military test pilots, but none of them had ever flown in Earth's orbit. Yes, they were chosen for this program and trained for the mission, but how prepared can you ever truly be to get launched into space for the first time in your life? None of them really knew what to expect or if they'd survive, but they took a chance to go higher, further, faster, and became the first American astronauts: the Mercury Seven. These real-life astronauts took a chance on a magnificent possibility, not knowing if they would fail or succeed. So, we might ask ourselves: What is keeping us from taking this leap of faith in our own lives?

I can't begin to tell you the amount of people—mostly women, especially Latinas—I know who don't dare show up for a job interview unless everything is completely aligned and they are letter-perfect. Deep down, they know they can do the job and would likely excel at it, so what's stopping them from jumping into this realm of possibility? Time and again, it all comes back to one single yet almighty emotion: fear. Fear of the unknown, fear of being unprepared, fear of not having what it takes, fear of making mistakes, fear of failure.

When we are little girls, our parents warn us: "Careful, don't run so fast, you might fall." "Watch out, that's dangerous!"

Those are the messages we start absorbing like sponges from the moment we take our first steps. Meanwhile, the boys are usually encouraged to run, to climb the tree, to jump from the swings. Boys are not only expected to take risks; they're also challenged to do so if they don't pursue them on their own. It's okay for them to fall because they're expected to get back up, dust themselves off, and move on to the monkey bars. Their bruises and scratched knees are celebrated with a quick hug and a pat on the back reassuring them that it's nothing, while girls are coddled and told to be extra careful next time so we don't fall again. Some may not even be allowed to try again. If you look into Captain Marvel's backstory, Carol's father decided to send her brother to college instead of her, believing that a woman's place was at home. Things are definitely changing now, but many adult women reading this book will likely be able to identify with some, if not all, of the dynamics previously described.

The ultimate message we've grown up hearing from family, society, and culture is that women are fragile and men are tough. We're told we must take extra precautions before doing anything, while men are encouraged to accomplish whatever they want. But that's not true. We can also climb that tree, fall, scrape our knees, and keep running higher, further, and faster. Carol Danvers didn't allow her father's beliefs to get in the way of her dreams. His imposed limitations pushed her to join the air force, pave a way for herself, and prove to her dad that she is just as tough and as good as the boys, if not better.

❬ ❬ ❬

The fear will continue to be there; it won't magically disappear. You'll feel it in your clenched stomach or racing heart, but what I want you to do is put it in a little box and give it a name. Make sure you acknowledge it daily, and talk to the box: *Good morning, Fear. I know you're there, but I'm not bringing you along with me today, okay?* Do your best to leave that little box behind when you walk out the door. As the Scarlet Witch says in *Captain America: Civil War*, "I can't control their fear. Only my own." You can't do anything about other people's fears, but you do have the power to get a grip on your own so that they don't pilot your life.

Next time a possibility presents itself—a job posting, an interview, a networking opportunity—show up regardless of how prepared you feel. I've seen men do this at countless meetings and interviews. They will take a seat at the table, get comfortable, and calmly steer the conversation to the 40 percent of their plan they can confidently cover rather than the 60 percent they're lacking. Women, on the other hand, show up and mention that they've got 97 percent of what is required for the job at hand and then quickly shift the focus to the 3 percent they *don't* have, to assure those in charge that they are ready to work extra hard to make up for that 3 percent. *Stop!* Please don't do this to yourselves. Your 97 percent is likely better than what anyone else has brought to the meeting. Forget about the 3 percent that prevents you from being perfect. I want to hear about the 97 percent that makes you the ideal candidate for this position. What's more, nobody—and I mean *nobody*—has it all. No one has a perfect combination of talent and capabilities; we all lack something, and that's what makes us perfectly imperfect humans. Next time you walk into a room, a meeting, an interview, please consider feeling confident that you already have what it takes to leap into the moment headfirst, and that whatever you may be lacking, you can learn along the way. I know this firsthand.

❮ ❮ ❮

Remember the job Alison's friend offered me? That was my first ever gig in production. I was hired as a production assistant (PA) for the additional photography shoot of a movie starring Christian Slater. After saying yes, I switched around some shifts at Alaska Airlines and Black Angus, and I was on set bright and early and ready to go on my first day as a PA. It was one of those gorgeous, sunny LA mornings that exuded good vibes. With a beaming smile, I eagerly walked over to the assistant director to get my assignment for the day. He greeted me and quickly got down to business. "You need to lock traffic today," he said matter-of-factly. My stomach did a cartwheel.

"Okay," I replied, completely clueless as to what that meant, "so how do I do that?"

"Just tell them to stop," he said as he gave me a small, black two-way radio with a short antenna and a knob that could tune to several channels.

My heartbeat turned into a drumroll as I grabbed the device and stared down at it, desperately trying to process how it worked.

"You've never done this before," he said.

"No," I replied honestly.

"Okay, press here, talk, let it go, and then wait for the answer."

"Got it."

It was around eight in the morning, the height of rush hour in LA. Thankfully we were off a one-way street intersection in a neighborhood that wasn't too busy. So I took my position on the corner, and when I heard the go-ahead on the radio—"Lock traffic!"—I confidently walked into the middle of the street, raised my hand, and stopped the cars. In Los Angeles, residents are used to seeing the large movie trucks parked in different areas and they know that means there's a film shoot happening, so they're generally quite patient. But as the minutes ticked by and the line of vehicles grew longer, a few drivers began to anxiously honk their horns. Unfazed by their restlessness, I turned to them and said, "Shhh, we're shooting." Nothing was going to stop me from getting my one assignment of the day done right. I heard the director yell, "Cut," but I didn't budge. A couple of minutes later, a guy got out of his car and yelled out, "Hey, you've gotta let traffic go now!"

"Why?" I replied.

"Because they yelled 'cut,'" he said.

I quickly glanced over to the other PA and realized he was allowing cars through. Puzzled, I looked back down my street, unsure of how to proceed, until a commanding voice on the radio said, "Victoria, release traffic."

"No, no. Jack told me to lock it," I replied.

"This is Jack. Release traffic."

"Are you sure?" I asked.

"Victoria, we only lock traffic while we're rolling and we release it when we say 'cut.'"

I instantly jumped out of the way, waving at the cars to signal they should drive by, while my mind went into a tailspin: *Oh my*

God, I'll never be asked back to this set! I couldn't believe I had screwed up on my first day, during my first shot as a production assistant. I was mortified, but then I took a deep breath and did my best to quell that voice in my head, determined to absorb as much as I could from this experience and focus on finishing the day knowing I had given it all I had. Instead of wallowing in my mistake and the fear of having failed on my first day ever on set, I took the feedback, adapted, adjusted, and kept at it regardless of how much I stumbled along the way. I was embarrassed for a minute but recovered quickly, and by the end of the day, after becoming an expert at locking traffic, the team asked me back to finish the following two days of shoots. Traffic never flowed better!

Whenever I got a call for a one-off job as a production assistant on a commercial or a film, I had to juggle my schedule and find someone to cover my shifts at Alaska Airlines, Black Angus, and Paramount. Being a page at Paramount was still fun to me, and I had only been at Black Angus for less than a year and loved being a server—there's something communal about feeding people; to this day, having friends and families come together to share a meal warms my heart—but Alaska Airlines was starting to wear on me. Airports and hospitals are two of the places that can bring out the best and worst of us. If you're there for positive reasons, it can be a pretty joyful experience, but if the circumstances weigh heavy on your heart, the atmosphere can become quite grim. And the ones who bear the brunt of these emotional swells at airports are usually the ticket counter agents.

I remember one shift in particular when we were dealing with a delayed flight due to weather conditions. Everyone was rightfully upset but taking it in stride, knowing it was beyond our control, except for one guy. When he first walked up to the counter demanding an explanation, his slurred words and erratic behavior clearly gave away that he'd had one too many drinks at the nearby bar.

"I'm sorry, sir," I replied in the calmest tone I could muster, "but we can't do anything about the weather."

He grumbled something and walked away, only to return a few minutes later with the same questions and demands.

I once again patiently replied, "Unfortunately, there's nothing we can do at this time. It's a safety issue due to extreme weather."

This drove him into a tirade. As his voice gained volume and his words turned abusive, alarm bells sounded in my head and my fight-or-flight response kicked in. The situation was escalating beyond my control. Suddenly, amid a wave of epithets I prefer not to repeat, the guy tightened his grip around the sleek metal briefcase in his right hand and swung it at my head. My adrenaline-induced reflexes kicked in, and I ducked behind the counter just in time to see a flash of silver sweep the space where I had just been standing. While the man lost his balance from the sudden exertion, I grabbed the phone and hastily called security. When the officers arrived on the scene a few minutes later and asked him to leave, he began to throw punches and became increasingly violent, so they handcuffed him and forced him to sit down.

"Sir, you have to stay this way until you sober up," said one of the officers.

Another one brought him coffee and added, "And by the way, once the storm passes and the plane can take off, you won't be allowed to board the plane until you apologize." Such a chance would probably not be given today, with airports so heavily secured and unruly passengers quickly put on the No Fly List, but that was not the case then.

The plane was delayed six hours. It took him five hours to say he was sorry, likely the amount of time he needed for the alcohol in his system to run its course. That day, as I drove home, I thought, *How much longer do I want to do this job?*

I hustled for a while, until I reached a point when I had to start turning down production work. That's when I knew the time had come to quit the three jobs I was juggling, which had gotten me this far, and focus solely on film production. Most production assistants were twenty years old—I was twenty-seven, a latecomer to the role, but my age made me more reliable and mature on the job, which was highly valued, so it worked in my favor.

I honestly didn't care what I was asked to do during my PA days because I was focused on pursuing this road and learning all the lessons I could along the way, no matter how seemingly trivial. Aside from locking traffic and cleaning up a ridiculous amount of garbage at the end of each day on different sets, one of my most important tasks early on was getting what we call "second meal." Per union rules, the cast and crew must be provided with breakfast, lunch, and, on days when a shoot runs later into the night, dinner, or as we call it, second meal. It's not a sit-down event. Everyone is eager to wrap up the day and go home, so this is intended to be a quick-and-easy, on-the-go bite to give the cast and crew one last hit of fuel to make it across the finish line. Pizza was always my first choice. I can't tell you how much I loved walking on set balancing boxes of hot pies in my arms and yelling, "Pizza's here! Pizza's here!" I smiled widely when each person took their slice, knowing that this would not only feed them but also gift them a few minutes of solace after a long and arduous day. Years later, while at Marvel, when we were working tirelessly to deliver a final cut, I remembered how that small dose of comfort could go a long way, so we made sure to bookend our work with doughnuts in the morning and pizza in the evening.

Leaping before you think you're ready is the first big step to actually *living* in the world of possibility. So if you're offered an opportunity that scares the hell out of you yet also thrills you, go for it. I never felt I couldn't do it. Even when it was an uphill climb, I laced up my boots and hiked to the base camp, gathered my thoughts and energy, and continued up the next trail until I hit my first summit. If it's something I want to do, sooner or later I will get it done. Half of what it takes to win any battle is showing up. That fear of rejection, of not being heard, of not having anything to contribute—put it in your little box and leave it at home, because just having *you* in a meeting already makes a difference. Your presence changes the dynamic and energy in the room. Trust your gut, stay true to who you are, jump in, show up, and get ready to say yes!

❮ ❮ ❮

One day, I found myself working as the production assistant on a three-day shoot for a Ridley Scott Associates (RSA) commercial where the visual effects were being handled by Digital Domain, a company founded by James Cameron, Stan Winston, and Scott Ross. I had heard of them before and was eager to continue learning and absorbing everything I could from each one of these experiences.

The beauty of starting at the bottom was that I could meander around different production departments and get a peek at what they did and how they functioned at each level. So, during my small windows of downtime, I strolled over to Digital Domain's crew and asked them a thousand questions: "Why do you do that?" "How does it work with the motion control rig?" "How does the rig talk to the data?" "Where do you put the data?" I loved getting to learn the technical aspect of filming. My curiosity has never known any bounds, and I always want to find the holes in a system and then figure out how to fill them. When we finished shooting that commercial, someone from Digital Domain approached me and asked if I'd consider working for them.

"Well, I don't know anything about visual effects," I replied honestly, unsure if this was the right path for me.

"No problem. We think you have a great attitude. Plus, you don't need to know much, it's a temporary position. We need someone to help the executive producer's assistant because she broke her leg."

I hesitated at first. I had already been working as an assistant production coordinator for a while, and I was eager to move on to the next step up the ladder and become production coordinator. But then it dawned on me: *I don't have another job lined up after this week.* Why not spend a couple of weeks at this renowned company with this supersmart group of people? I could take the time to learn some visual effects basics and get paid and fed. Once it was over, I could continue pursuing a production coordinator role. So I set aside my hunger for a new title, focused on the bigger picture, and said yes.

On my first day, I walked into this company's workplace—a massive warehouse now home to Google's offices in Venice, California—and was led to the executive producer's office. His assistant was sitting at a desk adjacent to his door. Even with her broken leg, she could work her desk just fine. What she needed help with the most was the fax machine, which was the main form of communication back in the 1990s. Messages, contracts, estimates, you name it, they came via fax. The problem was that the company's fax machine was located near the front of the building, almost a block away. So I spent the first day on the job basically running back and forth from the machine to the assistant's desk either sending or receiving faxes. There was a clear gap in this process, and I felt an overpowering urge to fill it. On my third day, I noticed there was a phone line next to the assistant's desk that was not being used. After checking to make sure the line was live, I made my way over to the building next door on a scavenger hunt–like mission and dug up an old fax machine. By the end of the day, I had everything set up and called over the assistant.

"I appreciate the opportunity to work here, but you don't need me to get the faxes on the other side of the floor anymore. I found this other fax machine, which works, and that line there next to your desk, which I tested and is good to go. All you have to do is use this number instead of the other one for faxes from now on.

Why pay me for more days when you have this simple solution?"

The executive producer, Ed Ulbrich, overheard me and came out of his office.

"Yes, let's use this fax instead," he said, "but you're not going anywhere."

And that was the beginning of my visual effects career. I stayed at Digital Domain for the next four years and continued to work with Ed throughout the years, including on the MCU films during my Marvel days.

At first, I bounced from one team to the next as a coordinator, and then, within the first year or so, I managed to become the company's most junior visual effects (VFX) producer. As I learned on the job, a VFX producer is in charge of the visual effects budget and the logistics of how to make anything that falls under visual effects happen. This can include smaller components, such as creating dust, fog, fire, and bullet hits that can later be used to composite a shot, or bigger visual effects, such as creating worlds, environments, and computer-generated characters. This involves working side by side with the director of photography, production designer, costume designer, prop master, stunt coordinator, special effects supervisor, and director to gather all the data and info we need to make sure that everything that is not currently there will later be built into the scenes as expected.

Last but not least, the VFX producer works alongside the VFX supervisor, the person who creatively designs and ushers the director's vision through preproduction, shooting, and post-production. At the beginning of my career in the early 1990s, VFX producers weren't usually at the table with those creating the scenes, but somehow I was allowed in and was one of the few who expressed a creative opinion, and I was lucky to work in teams that valued my fresh take and input. Today, VFX producers are very much a part of the creative process.

So how did I land that position so quickly in my budding career? Anytime one of my colleagues said "Oh, that's a hard director to work with" or "Oh, the location is too far away," I chimed in and said, "I can do it." Sure, I was taking their leftovers—the difficult directors, the remote locations, the more complicated computer-generated and 3D projects—but I saw them as golden nuggets with which I could eventually create my own bar of gold and jump-start my career. Even though I was still learning on the fly, they trusted me because they knew that if I came up against something I didn't understand, I had no problem saying, "I don't know, but let me figure it out and I'll get back to you." I am eternally grateful to every brilliant mind who was willing to share their knowledge with me. I asked so many questions all the time! But it was due to their generosity with their knowledge that I eventually managed to help our team maximize our time by reassembling the workflow, thereby getting ahead of the curve and keeping our clients happy.

€ € €

Everyone has had to go through their own learning curve in their careers at some point. Just because you don't know how to do something doesn't mean you can't learn it. What's more, you may think you need to have every answer, but once you've learned them all, the questions will change, and you'll be back to square one. So I urge you to claim not knowing something with confidence. Have the basic tools at your disposal and then build your kit along the way. After more than thirty years on this path, I'm still learning every single day. That's what keeps my passion alive for this career—as producers, we are constantly learning and evolving together with the creativity of our peers and the help of technology.

TV commercials were my side door into Hollywood, but my goal was to work in film. After more than four years at Digital Domain, I requested to be moved to the feature film division, but I was told I didn't have enough experience in that area.

"But it's just a format issue, isn't it?" I asked. We weren't doing it digitally at the time, so it was really a matter of volume and format.

"Nope, you can't do it yet. You just don't have the experience," replied the film department's executive producer.

If experience was what I needed, then that's what I would get—higher, further, faster! Soon after that conversation, I interviewed for a visual effects production manager and line producer position at DreamWorks, and in 1997 I got hired to work on *Shrek*. It was the first time I worked with intangible characters who could realistically emote, and I thought, *Wow, we can do this with animation? We can actually make someone feel something through our software and creative collective?* That's when it really hit me for the first time: The visual effects and animation teams had the power to make anything out of nothing. Say you're shooting a real-life restaurant scene. Everything you need is right there: the table, chairs, patrons, servers, trays, food. The scene you need is within the environment and location you choose. It's pretty straight-forward. So when I began to encounter scenes that required us to create magic to fill in the blanks of the imagination, that was when my role made me giddy with innovation and inspiration.

I remember feeling this thrill again a few years later, while working as a visual effects producer on Tim Burton's *Big Fish*. When I watched the scene where Ewan McGregor first sees Alison Lohman across the circus tent and everything stops, frozen in time, and he maneuvers around the different big top acts—the popcorn suspended in midair falling to the ground as he pushes it aside on his way toward her—it took my breath away. To think this all began with someone putting the scene on the page, followed by a team of brilliant minds who imagined this moment and helped create a metaphor of love, of crossing all obstacles, big and small, to get to the person on the other side of the room ... what a magical and whimsical way to portray the hurdles we face when seeking love. In hindsight, it wasn't a big deal to create that specific digital element, to have the popcorn floating around him, but the emotional add-on took it to the next level. It made me realize that what seems impossible is actually possible, and it cemented my career path. *As a storyteller, if I can do that,* I thought, *while also helping create a story that will make the world a better place, I think it will be a life worth living.*

Nowadays, sound and images are the language I can relate to the most, but back then, I was still in the learning trenches. I didn't have any mentors on my way up. I had my curiosity, my continuous stream of questions, and a group of digital and visual effects supervisors willing to teach me the ins and outs of this fascinating world. Pretty much everything I've done has been following the footsteps of men who have done it before me, men whom I admired and who were generous with their knowledge, but there were very few women around, so I had to figure out how to make this journey my own. I was winging it, trusting my gut, taking leaps, forging my own path.

Nevertheless, when I get asked if I had any role models, people I looked up to, the answer that first crosses my mind is Kathy Kennedy. The first time I saw Kathleen Kennedy's name was on an *E.T.* movie poster back in Argentina—she had recently cofounded the production company Amblin Entertainment with Steven Spielberg and Frank Marshall, and *E.T.* was her first film as a producer. And I remember thinking, *Wow, there's a woman there. E.T. has a woman producer.* As the years went by, her name continued to appear in the movie credits I eagerly read on films. She soon became associated with other movies that are now considered classics, like *The Color Purple, Schindler's List,* and the Indiana Jones and Jurassic Park franchises. My admiration only grew stronger when I became a producer myself. She turned into a type of silent mentor in my eyes, a trailblazing figure I looked up to and could identify with even though I'd never met her.

The process of becoming a successful female VFX producer in Hollywood felt like driving down a desolate road in a barren landscape. I knew of a few other women on the same track, but it almost felt like we existed in the multiverse, living parallel lives. And on set—other than for costume, and hair and makeup—there were no other female heads of department, let alone female film producers. What's more, at the beginning of my career in the

1990s, the role of VFX producer, for women at least, was very much administrative, and many of the men in the industry had a hard time seeing us as equals. Oftentimes, we'd be treated more like assistants or the ones who could put together meetings, and I found myself thinking, *No, I figure out how to put your vision through, and by doing that, I'm helping you see all the details you might be overlooking trying to see the forest for the trees.* I would've loved to have another female VFX producer to talk to about these and other experiences as they happened, but, although we knew of one another's existence, we weren't in touch. Thankfully, the lines of communication have now opened up among visual effects producers, and there is a true sense of camaraderie that helps us all survive this jungle together.

When my role model Kathy Kennedy became the president of Lucasfilm in 2012, our worlds had fewer degrees of separation because Marvel is one of Skywalker Sound and Industrial Light & Magic's key clients. One day, my friend Lynwen Brennan, general manager and executive vice president of Lucasfilm, said, "We should set up a time for you to meet Kathy." My heart skipped a beat. When Lynwen called a little later to confirm our lunch meeting, I was so over the moon, I hopped on my kick scooter at the office and glided down the hallways of the entire second floor of the Frank G. Wells Building on the Walt Disney Studios lot. As I rode by rows of cubicles, offices, conference rooms, and the communal area, I rang my bell and yelled at the top of my lungs, "I'm meeting Kathy Kennedy! I'm having lunch with *Kaaathyyy Kennedyyy!*" When I approached the office of Kevin Feige, producer and president of Marvel Studios, on my scooter, the commotion brought him to the door, and he asked me, "What's going on, Victoria?"

"I'm having lunch with Kathy Kennedy!" I whispered back like a little girl about to meet her favorite superhero. "She's, like, my favorite producer *ever*!"

"What?!" he exclaimed in pretend offense.

"Well, my favorite *female* producer ever," I corrected myself, laughing excitedly.

At this point, I had actually met Kathy briefly twice before, once in Steven Spielberg's office and another time at the Oscars when she was nominated for *The Curious Case of Benjamin Button* and we were nominated for *Iron Man* visual effects. She didn't remember this, but I sure did.

When the day of our lunch finally arrived, I walked into Ivy at the Shore in Santa Monica, heart racing and a smile slapped across my face. During the first twenty minutes, I sat across from my hero and out of my mouth came an Iguazú-size waterfall of compliments. I gushed about what she had meant to me as I came up in my career, what she meant to women all over the world, how she inspired so many of us. I could hardly catch my breath, and all the while, she nodded and smiled and slowly began to sink deeper into her seat, looking more and more embarrassed. But having daydreamed of the moment I could say all of this to her, I pressed on. Until her eyes started to well up.

"Okay, I'm not going to make you cry," I said, changing gears. "Now I'm going to tell you everything that is wrong with your company."

She let out a chuckle, and that snapped us both back to our

lunch-meeting reality. We went on to talk about our processes and how to make things better, and those two hours together became the start of a wonderful friendship. People say "Never meet your heroes," but I couldn't disagree more; I say take the leap, show up, say yes, and meet your heroes.

❮ ❮ ❮

At the end of the day, if I hadn't considered accepting a job I knew nothing about, and hadn't set aside my ego and said yes to keeping the same title for a while, I wouldn't have gotten the job at Digital Domain. And if I hadn't taken that job, I wouldn't have embarked on a career of thirty-plus years as a visual effects producer—a path that, with time and tireless work, led me to becoming one of the presidents of a very influential studio of global renown, a job I had never done until the opportunity presented itself and I jumped in headfirst. But I'm getting ahead of myself.

My point is that if someone offers you a shot, take it, even if you don't have all your ducks in a row. If that person can see your potential, so should you. Lead with a yes. Jump even if you don't feel 100 percent ready. Superheroes don't have it all figured out at the start of the movie. We see them tread through their own struggles, lessons, and budding ingenuity, and that makes their wins all the sweeter.

As you move along your path, make sure to always remain in a constant state of discovery. Don't confuse motion with progress. A rocking horse moves back and forth but remains in the same place. One thing is the illusion of motion, and the other is the truth of progress. Remember: The fastest route is not always the straight line. Look up to others, observe how they did it—and then pave your own way, walk in your own shoes at your own pace, and create an experience that is unique to you and only you. We are not all one and the same, but we are all capable of going higher, further, faster, baby!

7

Compromise Where You Can, but Define Your Nonnegotiables

"Compromise where you can. Where you can't, don't.
Even if everyone is telling you that
something wrong is something right.
Even if the whole world is telling you to move,
it is your duty to plant yourself like a tree, look
them in the eye, and say, 'No, you move.'"

—SHARON CARTER QUOTING MARGARET CARTER,
CAPTAIN AMERICA: CIVIL WAR **(2016)**

Even before I came up in the film business, my overriding philosophy has always been to say yes. The word *no* automatically closes the doors to unforeseen opportunities. *Yes* opens those doors and allows you to poke your head inside and see if that road is right for you. However, sometimes you may find roads that could be right *if certain conditions are met first*. That's when I like to say "Yes, but . . ." I believe everything is negotiable, yet we all should draw the line somewhere. The key is to know where that line is for you, so you will be ready to clearly express your nonnegotiables when the time comes. Those are your choices to make, the ones that look out for your best interests in work and in life, the ones that will lead you to a better path forward.

The list of nonnegotiables shouldn't be long; keep it as close to one or two items as possible. Never start the conversation with your nonnegotiables, because that's like beginning the talk with a limitation. Listen, digest the information you receive, compromise where you can, and if you feel you've hit your nonnegotiable item, then bring that up and take the necessary actions to keep your integrity intact.

When I first started out in the industry, I was working on commercials, but my sights were set on film production, which is why, as I've mentioned, after four years, I decided to leave Digital Domain to pursue this dream. Unbeknownst to me, that was my first ever nonnegotiable in my career. Once I landed a job on a film, my goal was to get visual effects producer credit. It wasn't an explicit nonnegotiable yet, but it definitely pushed me to choose films where this possibility lived. When I worked on *Shrek*, for example, it took us quite some time to get it off the ground, and I was all in. But (there's that *but* I was talking about!) when one of the studios decided to take it to Pacific Data Images (PDI) in San Francisco, I decided to step away from this project. I had just bought a house in Los Angeles, and even though I was fascinated by this film and its possibilities from a visual effects perspective, I didn't want to move, and even less so for a project that wouldn't guarantee me a producing credit. I was eager to get my career off the ground, and to do so I knew my name needed to start showing up on-screen.

Meanwhile, I had found out that Peter Jackson was looking for a VFX producer for *The Lord of the Rings: The Fellowship of the Ring.* I loved the idea of working on that film, so I hopped on a plane and flew to New Zealand to interview for the job. When I saw esteemed visual effects producer Eileen Moran was also there, I knew she was a shoo-in for the position. While in the waiting area, she leaned over and said, "Victoria, if I get this, would you take over my current movie?" I said, "Yes." And that yes led me to work for Rhythm & Hues Studios on *The 6th Day,* where I received my first visual effects producer credit. Then I did another one with them, *Cats & Dogs,* with credit too. And I was off to the races.

❝ ❝ ❝

A couple of years later, while working on *Big Fish,* which went into turnaround for a long time—meaning it took forever to reach the preproduction phase for many different reasons—I was asked to fly to Australia and help out on *Darkness Falls,* which was facing some issues. I didn't want to do it. There was a chunk of work coming to Sony Pictures Imageworks for *The Lord of the Rings,* and I was eager to jump on the opportunity of working on, at the very least, a piece of this film.

"Just give me that," I said.

"No, no, we need someone like you to travel to Australia and make sure this film gets back on its feet. The movie is over budget, it's a bit of a mess."

"Okay, I'll go," I said.

Compromise was a huge part of what continuously pushed me forward on my path. Interestingly enough, while in Sydney, doing a job that I had initially not wanted to take on, I met the woman who I'd fall madly in love with and would later become my wife. You never know what will come out of just one simple *yes.*

❬ ❬ ❬

For the first ten years of my career, I worked as a VFX producer at different facilities and traveled across Europe, Asia, the Americas, and Africa. One of the most exciting trips I remember from early on was for a commercial we shot in Reykjavík, Iceland. The location for the commercial was at one of Iceland's famous geysers. Most of the geysers on the planet are located in five countries, and not all expel an impressive jet of hot water and steam into the air frequently enough to catch on camera during one day of filming. So we went to the one that had the best chances of erupting several times an hour to catch the perfect shot.

We set up near this enormous vent-like crater in the Earth's surface that sporadically spouted a flow of steam into the atmosphere and peered out from fully covered faces into the open, volcanic landscape that was skirted by deserted hills lined with sparse rows of barren trees. The scene was so far-flung from my everyday LA life, I was stricken by wonder. We had a truck that held warm water on location, but it was so cold, each time water was expelled from the tank, it turned into snow. Meanwhile, the freezing temperatures made the cameras constantly lock up, which added an extra layer of stress because they needed to be ready to go at a moment's notice to catch the geyser in action.

After several takes and a lot of waiting around, we were finally able to call it a day. I can still feel the icy wind on my back contrasted by the warmth of the sudden, fleeting burst of boiling water and steam from the majestic land of fire and ice.

The ensuing ten years were a thrilling ride packed with fascinating, potent experiences like the one in Iceland, and my insatiably curious mind was hooked, but it also meant that I was on the road nine months out of each year. I had managed to buy a house along the way, but I had yet to see a sunset from my window. Each time I walked in, night had already fallen on Los Angeles and I had to pat the walls in the pitch-dark entryway to find the right switch to turn on the one light that led me straight to my bedroom. I had some basic pieces of furniture and several lamps—though they had no light bulbs, because I never used them. By sunrise, I was out the door and back in my car heading to the airport.

I loved all the traveling—I was able to see more of the world. But after a few years it started to feel like I was a feather in the air, floating from one set and hotel to the next. Different time zones. Arrivals. Departures. No sense of home. But I kept going because I was building my résumé, chasing jobs, thriving, learning, gathering invaluable experience, working with amazing people, and then moving into a VFX producer role, which would mean managing the entire process of creating VFX for a film rather than managing the production through a facility. This opportunity finally came with Ridley Scott's *Kingdom of Heaven*. I put every ounce of energy and brainpower toward this project, pushing my body to the limit to help bring the film to fruition. We were shooting in several cities in Spain and Morocco and posting in London.

On location in Morocco, while shooting in a small city called Ouarzazate known as the gateway to the Sahara, the elements at times became overpowering. As our crew built an enormous castle and 1,500 king's men waited on the sidelines for their cue, the temperatures soared past one hundred degrees Fahrenheit and oftentimes we were hammered with dust storms, so much so that we had to wear goggles all day to protect our eyes. Every inch of our bodies was covered to give us respite from the heat and dust, but sand still worked its way into every crevice of our bodies. By the end of the day's shoot, back at the hotel, when I peeled off my clothes, grains of sand sprinkled to the floor as if I'd spent the entire day at the beach.

One evening, as I was driving back to the hotel from this set, eager to take a long shower and put my feet up, I realized I didn't have enough gas to get to my destination. I was notorious for not filling up my tank whenever I had a car on location—I always left it to the last minute. Morocco was no different. But in this case, I was driving down an isolated road with no gas station in sight. Stepping out of my car to ask for help at sunset without the appropriate attire covering me in this predominantly Muslim country was not an option for me. The last thing I wanted to do was dis-respect or offend anyone. So I grabbed the brick-size cell phone plonked on the passenger's seat and called the production team for guidance. I explained where I thought I was located based on some nearby landmarks—I couldn't read the signs, and I couldn't take a picture because our phones didn't have that capability at the time.

"Head south and look for a billboard with a picture of the king," they said. "As soon as you pass that billboard, you'll find a gas station to your left."

I hung up and followed the directions, but after passing the billboard, there was nothing in sight. So I called the team again, who repeated the directions, to no avail. "It's getting late, why don't you just come get me?" I suggested, feeling unease settle in as the sun was no longer visible on the horizon. I wasn't too far from the set yet, so they arrived pretty quickly with gas in tow. Once we were back on the road, we passed no less than eight bill-boards featuring the king, and we all started chuckling. I would have never found that gas station! Only now do I realize how much we accomplished filming movies across the world in the 1990s and early 2000s without the technology we have today. The arrival of widely accessible GPS systems and smartphones was a game changer!

I was on the road for almost nineteen months during the film-ing of *Kingdom of Heaven*, all the while trying to keep my budding relationship afloat by taking the Friday red-eye to London to spend the weekend with my girlfriend only to jump on the Sunday red-eye and head straight back to work on Monday. I was hopping around from one place to the next so often that one morning I opened my eyes and looked around the dimly lit, nondescript room, unable to recognize my surroundings. *What day is it?* I thought as I sat up in the bed. *What city am I in now?*

After you've stayed in a room for a few days, you begin to get your bearings, you know how to get to the bathroom in the dark. But when you're skipping from city to city and country to country every other day, it is incredibly bewildering to the senses. I was smack in the middle of the infamous rat race many of us know so well, unable to see it because it had become second nature. It felt like if I stopped, my world might collapse, so I kept going, until one day my body said, *Enough is enough. Victoria. If you don't stop, I will do it for you.*

The pounds had started piling on, my thyroid was out of whack, and upon my return home, during a time that was supposed to be a much-needed break between films, I was diagnosed with shingles. Suddenly, the R & R I had hoped to enjoy during those precious weeks off became an incredibly stressful period in my life. And in that moment, it hit me: Something wasn't working. My body was screaming at me to stop and pay attention. When I did, I realized it wasn't just the physical toll that was bringing my life to a screeching halt—I wasn't 100 percent happy; I wasn't in a good place. The job had taken everything out of me, and my nomadic life was no longer bringing me joy. Something had to give.

I had traveled the world, had built a career from nothing, and had managed to land jobs with my bucket list of top-of-the-line directors, from Ridley Scott to Tim Burton, but now all I wanted to do was stay home. So, once *Kingdom of Heaven* wrapped, I decided it was time to put myself and my relationship first and course correct. I lost weight, got my shingles under control, worked on rebalancing my thyroid, and in the process redefined my nonnegotiables. Instead of choosing my projects based on my go-to list of directors, I chose me. It was time to get back on track to health and happiness. I decided I would only do movies that shot in Los Angeles for the foreseeable future. That was my new nonnegotiable. Nothing more, nothing less. I loved my work, but it was time for me to do it near my home for a change.

There will come a time when you will have to choose yourself and make yourself a priority over your job, especially in the film industry. If you don't, Hollywood (much like the corporate world) will home in on what they need from you, drain it out of you, and suck you dry without batting an eyelid. Hollywood is a machine. It needs its parts to continue functioning. When you are no longer of use, it will move on, like you do at the airport, to the next available agent. As difficult as it may be to understand, it's not personal. Knowing this gives you the power to realize that there are other possibilities, other ways of playing this game, and the choice is yours for the taking.

With that in mind, as I got my health in order, I turned down two big movies that were shooting in Europe. It wasn't easy to say no to those fantastic directors, but I knew that if I pushed myself any further, my health would likely suffer much worse consequences, so I stuck to my nonnegotiable. Then I received a call from Sony. They were working on a movie called *Tonight, He Comes* (later renamed *Hancock*), and they needed a VFX producer on board.

"Where does it shoot?" I asked.

"It shoots in LA."

"Okay, I'll do it," I replied.

That's where I met then film producer Louis D'Esposito. Despite being very different people, we hit it off right away. Banter was our thing, and although we often disagreed, we managed to find common ground despite our differences and laughed our hearts out in the process. We always challenged each other and pushed ourselves to grow, and we both knew how to make stuff happen, so working together felt right. With time, Lou became my work brother and he saw me as his "soul sister."

We went through two or three directors on *Hancock*, and then the movie got shut down temporarily. During this time, Louis called me one day and said, "Hey, I'm gonna do this movie with this director that I've worked with before—"

"Just tell me one thing," I said, interrupting him. "Where does it shoot?"

Louis paused for a second, slightly taken aback, as he was aware that I usually liked to hear more details about the film and its director. "It shoots in LA," he said.

"Great, then let me know where to be and when, and I'll see you there."

Louis asked me to meet him at a production office in Beverly Hills located above a Mercedes-Benz dealership. When I arrived, I saw a sign that said MARVEL, but I didn't really think anything of it at the time. I honestly didn't know that Marvel made movies. Oblivious to the connection, I walked into the elevator and a six-foot-tall man stepped in right after me. I glanced his way and thought his face was somewhat familiar, but I couldn't quite pin-point it, which is not unusual in LA.

"Good morning," he said, politely.

"Good morning."

"Are you going to the second floor?" he asked, noticing the button had already been pushed.

"Yes," I replied.

"Are you going to see Lou?"

"Yes, I am. Are you?" I asked.

"Yes, I am," he said.

The doors of the elevator slid open, and he walked out and veered right while I turned left. I glanced his way, a little puzzled, but figured he was going to the restroom. When I stepped into Louis's office, he greeted me warmly and said, "Let's go meet the director."

We walked down the hall and into the conference room, where Louis introduced me to Jon Favreau.

"Ah, there's the elevator girl!" he exclaimed warmly. "You didn't know who I was, did you?"

"I had no idea," I said, laughing. "First of all, I didn't think you were that tall."

He chuckled, and after some small talk, I finally asked, "Okay, so what movie are we doing?"

"It's called *Iron Man*," said Jon.

"What is that? What's *Iron Man*?"

"It's a superhero movie," he replied.

"Oh, okay."

"Do you like superhero movies?" he asked.

"I like movies that shoot in LA!" I said, smiling wide. Then I looked at Louis and asked, "It does shoot in LA still, right?"

"Yes, it shoots in LA," he replied.

"Great, let's do it!"

That's how the Marvel Cinematic Universe came a-knocking on my door in 2006. I didn't even like superheroes at the time—I liked that it shot locally and I liked working with Louis, and that's all that mattered. So I was ready to take on the job and do whatever was needed.

Getting caught up with everyone else's needs can become an enormous distraction that may keep you from seeking your own joy. The moments in my journey when I finally quieted the world around me and listened to my own needs have created the necessary space for me to make the greatest decisions of my life. This was one of them, and it all came down to realizing that I had to hang up my nomadic hat for a while and prioritize my well-being—a decision that ultimately allowed me to not just accept a job at Marvel, despite not having read the comics, but also marry my long-time girlfriend and say yes to the possibility of adopting our daughter, thus solidifying our family. All the pieces of my life that had been frozen in midair, like the popcorn in that *Big Fish* circus scene with Ewan McGregor, were now falling into place.

Had I not pushed the reset button on my life and defined this new nonnegotiable, I probably would have never considered the possibility of working on *Iron Man*. But I chose to say yes. I chose to give this superhero life a go. I figured it was my chance to dive in and discover why so many kids looked up to these characters, why so many adults cherished these heroes. What did they see in them? Why didn't I get it? I chose to remain open to the possibilities of these characters. And, as we began prepping *Iron Man* in 2006 and I became profoundly familiar with Tony Stark, I began to realize that the connection, the real pull, went beyond admiring the capes or shields or bionic arms or faster-than-light speed. At the end of the day, they all have their own craters to deal with, they all face moments when they need to jump before they think they're ready, and they all have to grapple with their identities in order to find their voice and step into their power. The more I learned about superheroes, the easier it was for me to relate to them. They won me over with their human qualities, which allowed me to stay in the conversation and be a part of their stories rather than observing from a distance. I was hooked. Now, after amassing more than thirty MCU productions to my name, I can honestly say: I never liked superheroes, but I liked *our* superheroes.

❮ ❮ ❮

Your nonnegotiables will evolve with the passing of time, and it will be up to you to redefine them and keep them handy as you forge ahead in your growth. If you know in your heart that you have earned a promotion or a raise or have the right experience for a job and the other party is simply not budging, you need to become a hound dog and sniff out the reasons why. Then see if the reasons you uncover make sense to you. If there's room for improvement on your end, then compromise, get it done, and come back again when you're better prepared. But if you don't agree, then it may be time for you to put your nonnegotiable on the table.

Like Kenny Rogers famously sings in "The Gambler," you have to know when to hold them, when to fold them, and when to walk away. That's right, when you've hit the line you're not willing to cross, when you bring up what you need to stay at a job (or in a relationship), you also have to be willing and able to walk away. Make your intentions clear. If they're convinced you won't leave, then you have to convince them that you will, and be prepared to follow through. I'm not encouraging you to cause a scandal—the last thing you want to do is burn bridges. But definitely be direct. Sit down and calmly let them know that you are hitting your limits, and if what you're asking for isn't taken seriously, then express that you are ready to leave. Doing so will give your nonnegotiable the weight it requires to be taken seriously. Make peace with the fact that by taking a stand there will be something gained and potentially something lost—it's not a given, but it could happen.

❦ ❦ ❦

I never dreamed of becoming an executive at a studio; producing has always been my thing. Leading a team makes me happy and proud. But once I entered the executive path at Marvel, I realized it gave me a chance to speak for more representation in our films and shows. That possibility is what eventually led us to consider the movie with the most diverse cast in the MCU: *Eternals*.

Released during the pandemic, when people were afraid of going to the theaters, it might not have been considered a box office hit by pre-pandemic metrics, but *Eternals* is a living and breathing success just by existing and having the most diverse cast become a part of the Marvel universe. If you look at the *Eternals* comic book cover, you'll see a group of white characters—no racial diversity, albeit three women and three men.

Since there was nothing in the comics that explicitly referred to the race of these characters, we searched for the perfect fit, opening the door to all actors.

In 2021—with *Eternals* only a few months away from its release date, and after working on twenty-five MCU films and spending the previous sixteen years doing more, more, more—I believed I had earned the right to the position of president of physical and postproduction, visual effects, and animation pro-duction. I had put it on the table to be considered a few times, but it hadn't happened yet. And I thought, *Okay, what's it all about, Alfie?* I began to seriously consider leaving but decided to bring it up with HR again. I was delighted to be a part of this group of people who made great movies that made a meaningful impact in many lives, but if this was to be the end of our road together, I was okay with that too. Thankfully, the money I make hasn't given me an overt sense of power—because I know one day it's here and the next it may not be. So my fight wasn't about money; it was about the title, the recognition of what I had contributed to the studio throughout the years. The greatest gift you can give anyone is the gift of time. And I didn't want to waste any more of it if I wasn't going to be aligned with what I thought I had earned years before. My nonnegotiable was now based on self-preservation, respect for myself, and my conviction to inspire others. I wanted young Latinas to look up and say, *Check it out, one of us is up there. One of us made it. One of us is at that table. If she can do it, so can I.*

In September 2021, I was officially offered the title of president of physical and postproduction, visual effects, and animation production, and I said yes.

❰ ❰ ❰

As you decipher your own nonnegotiables along your path, keep in mind that what worked for me might not work for you. Hollywood is a bit of a crapshoot. There is no "how to make it" formula—that's also what's so fascinating and inviting about this industry. Success can happen to anyone. Perseverance, flexibility, curiosity, integrity, and passion for what you do, those are the key components to keep close to your heart as you forge ahead.

I honestly believe that when you love what you do, work is not work. That's why I stayed at Marvel Studios for so long. I had yet to find another place in the world where I could tell the stories I wanted to tell with such meaningful and widespread global impact. That was a privilege I was fully aware of and remembered when I had to get through eighteen- to twenty-hour workdays. Every day, I woke up thinking, *Let's see how I will have fun today with what I'm doing.* That helped me lighten the load of responsibility. Now, if you wake up in the morning and don't feel like giving your all for what you love and believe in, then you may need to rethink your path and make the necessary adjustments to find that passion. Production can throw your life for a loop with its long and arduous hours, so those who work in this department usually do so because they wholeheartedly love it.

What's more, during some of my toughest times, work was the

place where I found solace. That's where I felt safe, loved, recognized, and appreciated. And sure, I put out fires daily, but I also jumped on my blue kick scooter and rang the bell as I rode across the office. I joked around with our team, I sang, I was loud, and my colleagues let me be me. No matter where I am, I like to bring joy to the long hours of the day and get as much life out of every project, every business trip, every person I meet, because that time spent doing what I love has the power to be incredibly fulfilling and inspiring if experienced through the right lens.

❮ ❮ ❮

With time and experience, my nonnegotiables once again shifted. Of course, I preferred to shoot in LA to be close to home, but it was no longer a deal-breaker. What has always mattered and continues to take front and center is my voice. I will only be where I am allowed to speak the truth, openly, out loud. My voice has consistently been my greatest asset, and being at Marvel gave me the room to flourish and speak for those who sometimes couldn't. This possibility allowed us to create space for a slightly better world and ultimately inspired me to stand firm for the chance to spread my wings and make room for a passion project outside of the MCU: *Argentina, 1985*.

As I came up in the business, many people asked me what stories I wanted to tell, and I always replied, "I want to make my version of *The Official Story*." That movie managed to publicly speak about a crucial and devastating time in Argentina. It opened the eyes of people in far-removed corners of the globe to our story, and it had an enormous impact in my life. I will never forget when Norma Aleandro's character begins to realize that her adopted daughter is likely the child of one of the many people who disappeared during the dictatorship and is probably one of the missing children who was kidnapped by the armed forces. It is a heart-wrenching film that brought widespread awareness to a treacherous time we hope will never be repeated.

So, when *Argentina, 1985* was brought to my attention, I immediately thought, *I have to do this movie. This is the story I've been saying I want to tell in film form since I started my career.* It was my chance to help give voice on a global scale to those who had been silenced during the military dictatorship, those whom I had marched for as a teenager in the streets of La Plata.

Argentina, 1985 is not a superhero story. It centers around a team of lawyers who take on some of the top military dictatorship participants during the renowned and critical 1985 Trial of the Juntas, which led to convictions of life in prison without parole. It's a story I needed to help tell because I suffered this dictatorship in the flesh. It's a piece of my past and my country's history, one that I want my daughter and all new and future generations to know and never forget, so that the world can learn from these atrocious times and never again stand by genocide.

I raised my voice and marched to demand justice then. And now I'm here to continue speaking up to help remind us, and those who come after us, of what can happen in our world if we stop protecting democracy . . . and how positive change *can* take place if we define our nonnegotiables and start using our voice.

8

Find Your Voice and Set Yourself Free

**"I've been fighting with one
arm tied behind my back.
But what happens when I'm finally set free?"**

—CAPTAIN MARVEL, *CAPTAIN MARVEL* (2019)

Silence is poison. It solidifies the moment before you, with possible detrimental effects. If we don't speak up, no one will ever know what we need, what we believe, what we are fighting for. And if our wants, needs, and convictions go unrecognized, creating real change in our lives and the world can become a near impossible task. It's like fighting with one arm tied behind our backs. After Carol Danvers comes to this realization with these all-important lines in *Captain Marvel*, she is able to unleash the full extent of her power. We may not have her superhuman strength or energy projection, but we are all born with a voice. That is your power. That is your antidote to silence. That is what can help you set yourself free.

I have always had a "big mouth" that I have used to openly express my opinions. Even when living under a military dicta-torship, I didn't consider shutting up. Yet I also know that life can get tricky, the craters can be hard to surpass, and because of that some may feel their voices quiet and may retreat to a safe corner. Many learn to put their heads down, do the work, and not cause a fuss along the way. Most want certain changes to take place in their lives or their surroundings but are afraid to speak up. However, for us to not use our voice is as poisonous as those who use theirs against us. It is up to us to dig this power out of the debris of our circumstances and at long last learn how to express ourselves to effectively advance change. I'm not talking about being disrespectful or insolent or saying whatever crosses your mind. The power of knowing *when* to speak up is an art; it takes time and requires practice. From a creative process stand-point, the key is to check before doing so to make sure your ideas or opinions aren't coming from a place of ego but rather a desire to improve the story. If your opinion is solely about putting the spotlight on yourself, then I would suggest keeping it to yourself. Should that idea get rejected, it will only lead to you feeling hurt and downcast on a personal level. Now, if the idea is for the story and it gets rejected, it won't be easy, but it's not personal. All you have to do is think about the feedback you received at the table and see if you can come back with something better.

As I've mentioned earlier, I get rejected all the time, and my ego is quite healthy. I don't take the noes I receive as others thinking I'm incompetent. Instead, I ask myself, *Does the idea not serve the story? Does it not work from that particular angle?* I aim to get to the why of that particular rejection to help reformulate my idea from a fresh perspective. Then I come to the next meeting with a "You were right on that front, it helped me see it from your perspective. With that in mind, what if we try to combine our ideas and do it this way instead?" Even if this new reformulated idea doesn't quite work either, at least it may help pave the way to one that will.

Having said that, there will be other fronts beyond the work process where you will want to make a point and will have to deal with the consequences, and other times when you will likely say far more by saying nothing at all. As you practice walking this fine line, you will make mistakes along the way. Instead of beating yourself up for those mistakes, do your best to learn from them so that you can do better next time.

I can't begin to count the times my circumstances have placed me in a position where my path has forked into two roads: Follow the group, or speak up. As you can probably gather by now, I usually choose to speak up, even when the odds are stacked against me. I can't help but think of this one time I was asked for my opinion at a work retreat, a few years before my Marvel days.

I was sitting at a table with some of the company's powers that be while they discussed the performance of someone who was not in that room. Everyone was voicing their opinion on the matter, and I was listening attentively, until they turned to me. "What do you think about this person, Victoria?" I looked around the table and thought, *Oh, wow, these people, who are more important and experienced than me, actually want my opinion.* I was still pretty green, and I felt flattered by their attention and honored that such a powerful group of people actually valued what I had to say. It fed my ego. I didn't understand the politics at play.

The person they were talking about, whom they were looking to fire, was actually someone I thought was awesome. I loved working with that person, and when it was my turn, I didn't shy away from expressing my honest opinion. I thought the other folks who also valued this colleague would express their feelings, but they all chose not to do it.

I have always spoken my mind and led with the truth and I always will, even if it goes against the general consensus in the room. However, as soon as the words flew out of my mouth, I noticed their pursed-lip reaction and instantly thought, *Shut up, just shut up!* I realized my opinion was being disregarded. I finished expressing myself, already knowing that what I had to say didn't matter. They only valued opinions that aligned with their own to back a decision they'd likely already made. But by the time I understood I had been played, it was too late.

I didn't have the foresight or experience to realize that if I went against the grain, it would likely turn me into "not a team player" in the eyes of those in power. I could've said *I have no opinion*, which was not true. I could've stayed quiet, but that would've gone against who I am. How do you get out of this conundrum unscathed? You don't. You either betray your integrity and follow the flock of sheep or you stick to your beliefs, speak the truth, and take the hit. Sometimes the "winning team" is not where you belong if it takes those tactics to score the win.

A few months later, when my contract was not renewed, which was a polite way of firing me, I knew exactly why. It wasn't a performance issue. It was an upper management core issue. I went back to that day and asked myself, *Did I make a mistake? Would I do it differently if I had the chance to be in the same room answering the same question?* And the honest answer is no. No, I don't regret speaking up. I would've said the same thing. Because I knew and believed, in my heart of hearts, what I said to be true. If I had followed the flock, my path might have been redefined. But it wouldn't have been the one I'm on now, because it no longer would've been mine. And down the road, I would've likely had to ask myself, *Where did you lose yourself? What happened to you? Who are you?* And I would've probably tracked it back to that day: *You betrayed yourself that day only to fit in, knowing deep inside you would never belong.* So, yes, I was temporarily out of a job, but my integrity remained intact.

As the years passed and my career expanded to new heights, I realized that I might not have been able to avoid that person's fate on the chopping block by speaking up, but I didn't betray my voice and my truth either. By saying no to them, I said yes to myself.

€ € €

If you're a woman in Hollywood, especially in the last thirty years, you've likely found yourself in rooms filled with men where your opinion was unrequired or ignored, or where you were assumed to be the girl who brought coffee and took notes. Rather than remaining complicit in the environment and old norms, I urge you to use your voice. Sometimes you'll find yourself with like-minded people; other times you may find yourself arguing with people you respect, yet despite the difference of opinion they will still want you there; and on other occasions you may find yourself in a pickle similar to the one I mentioned earlier, with colleagues who decide to oust you for defying their modus operandi. In the latter case, I urge you to ask yourself, *Is this the table I really want to be at?*

To answer that question, first think about this: Do you feel you aren't being heard when you speak up at the table, or are you not speaking up because you are self-censoring? Sometimes we remain quiet because we automatically think, *Oh, they don't want to hear from me.* Other times we believe there's no room for our opinion. Both of these thoughts may be true, but the only way we will know for sure is by actually voicing an opinion and honestly observing the reactions around the table. I don't suggest you go against the grain just for the sake of it; I'm talking about voicing an opinion that can help improve the story or project on the table. Don't be afraid to speak up, and don't be afraid of being judged. Remember, if you've been invited to the meeting, that's a clear sign the other attendees likely expect and welcome your opinion, so don't let that opportunity go to waste.

Once you've started to use your voice in meetings, I want you to start thinking about what you want now. Is there anything at work you resent not getting at this point in your career? If so, did you ever ask for it? When was the last time you asked for something that you believed you deserved but weren't getting?

From what I've observed throughout my years in this industry, a lot of women get paid less because they don't ask for more. In Hollywood, if you don't ask, you will not receive. What's more, if you don't ask, you'll never know what you could've accomplished. Not knowing creates a parallel what-if universe that occupies valuable real estate in your mind.

A colleague I mentor has more than twenty years of experience to her name, yet she recently found out she was making 35 percent less than a guy working at the same company with fifteen years of experience. The difference could have been based on their levels of performance, of course, but when she finally gathered the courage to speak up and ask why she wasn't receiving equal pay, the answer was much simpler than expected: He asked for a raise every year. She didn't. She was baffled. "I earned it as much as he did," she told them. The answer was "Yes, but you didn't ask for it." I wish this was the only time I've heard this story, but I've come across similar scenarios way more than I'd like to admit. I can't help but think of an idiom in Spanish: El que no llora, no mama; in other words: *The squeaky wheel gets the grease.* Don't linger in the resentment of what you don't get if you haven't asked for it.

So start squeaking, llorá, speak up, ask for what you deserve. You might just get it!

Many people blame their bosses for not giving them promotions or raises, but the possibility and responsibility of getting what we want starts with us. Your boss has a lot of other people to consider; you're not the only one they have on the roster. Stop conceding your power to someone else and then using that as a crutch to justify what you haven't been able to achieve. It's not fair to your boss, and it's not fair to you. I get a number of calls from people looking for advice who tell me, "Oh, I don't know how to ask for this." And all I say to them is "Ask, just ask. Be direct: 'I want a raise.' 'I want to do that job.' 'I don't want to do that movie, I want to do this movie.'" And then use solid reasons to back your request. I am always bewildered by the huge gap that exists between what we want in our minds and what we are able to communicate that we want. It's as if an invisible boulder with the word *deserve* carved on it rolls in the middle of our path and blocks us from the ask. If we feel we deserve it when we think of it, why don't we deserve it when we attempt to ask for it? Perhaps that's a question you can consider next time you are about to ask for something you know you have earned.

In the film business, higher-ups are usually playing a game of chess, constantly trying to fit people into the right place to get a project off the ground. If you don't speak up, they might not even realize they have the perfect person already within their company. Don't expect your bosses to know everything about you. People often make assumptions of who we are right away. And a lot of the time, those assumptions are wrong. So it's up to us to speak up, tell them who we are, and show them what we are capable of doing. When you open up and share your interests, goals, and what you want, that helps the decision makers see you in a new light and consider you for other possibilities.

The power of your own voice should be used to express your wants *and* to speak up when you believe you're not being treated fairly. I encourage women to take a stand when they feel they're being treated unfairly and are not being paid equally. Yet I also know it takes a lot of courage to stand up to your boss and your work family. Every family has to deal with conflicts. Some are messier than others, but sometimes it's necessary to go there in order to be heard and resolve feelings of discomfort and resentment. The power of your own ask allows that quiet voice in your mind to take center stage and do something for you. The more we do that for ourselves, the less we'll need others to do it for us, and the less we'll resent them for doing nothing at all. Your personal and professional life is no one else's responsibility but your own.

In Hollywood, there are many people who will take your calls and try to help out. In the hundreds of calls I've returned, I have gathered some helpful tips on what I have found can make a call successful:

- *Be mindful* of the person's valuable time.
- *Be honest and direct* about why you're reaching out.
- *Be specific* so you are prepared to make the most of your call or meeting.

Keep your opening short and to the point because time is of the essence. The person on the other end of the call will likely appreciate the flattery, but their time is valuable. They are gifting you this time, so don't waste the twenty minutes they've given you in telling them how wonderful they are or acting like you want to be their friend when you actually want something else out of this connection. You can share your admiration if there is any, but get to your ask right away.

Do your homework, and let them know within the first five minutes of the call or meeting why you decided to reach out:

I'd like to learn this from you. I have a specific question about the industry that I think someone with your expertise may be able to help me answer. I'm facing this issue and would love your advice. I have this idea I'd like you to consider.

Once you've got the person's attention, please be specific. If you call asking them for a job, their first response will likely be *You need to define what job you want.* Just asking for a job is like telling them *I want to be an explorer!* Okay, an explorer of what? Of the world? Great, then you need to map it out and create your itinerary. If that's the conversation you have, sure, the person you're calling may share a few good ideas, but they won't give you any type of job offer or lead. Don't make them do that first round of work for you. Have your résumé ready, think about the one or two things you'd like to get out of your interaction with that person, and stay focused on those points. Think about it. If you came to me having already done this preliminary work, knowing what country or city you want to explore first, then I would have the information I need to point you to the must-see neighborhood or streets, or to the people you need to meet in those spots, and you will end up getting so much more from that call. Make sure to relay a better understanding of what you're seeking and how you think the other person may potentially be able to help you so they can guide you in that direction.

And if you're lost, then come out and just say it: *I am lost.* That level of honesty is very helpful. You can spend twenty minutes masking the fact that you are lost, or you can spend that precious time searching for a road that will lead to finding your way.

Using the power of your voice to ask for what you want

usually takes courage that is mustered up with time. So when you're finally ready to make your ask, all you'll want to hear is *yes, yes, yes*. Since you've already been prepping for this moment for a while, there may be no room for a *no* in your mind.

But just as you took your time to get to this point, those you are asking may also need time to give you their answer. It's like coming out to your family. You do it when you feel strong and ready. It's a big moment that may have taken you months or years of preparation, so you can't help but expect your family to be okay with it right away. Of course, that would be ideal, but the reality is that sometimes families don't react as expected; they need more time to process this information, and that's okay too.

The act of speaking up or asking, on its own, won't guarantee you will get what you want. You are just as likely to get a *no* as you are to get a *yes*. It's what you do with that *no* that matters the most. Don't let it deter you from your purpose. Rejection is part of the journey. Keep asking. Keep expressing yourself. Keep moving forward. Even if you get denied, the act of speaking up and using your voice will have already helped you plant a seed in the other person's mind. And that's invaluable and empowering in and of itself because it means you have managed to cross that line and finally use your voice. Asking is a muscle. If you don't use it, it won't grow.

The noes I have received throughout my career have actually helped shape it. When I wanted to leave Digital Domain's commercial division to work in their film department, I was told I didn't have enough experience. That no pushed me to leave that job in search of the experience I was lacking, and I ended up developing a thriving career as a film visual effects producer. Then, when I wanted to produce films, not just the visual effects, I did my homework and found examples of two men who had followed a similar path. One of them was Kurt Williams, a VFX producer who had received a coproducer credit on *X-Men: The Last Stand*. I had that precedent in my back pocket to counter a possible no as I geared up to ask for coproducer credit for *Iron Man*, my first Marvel film. I hadn't just overseen the visual effects in that movie; I had also been a part of the production team, working alongside Louis D'Esposito and Kevin Feige. So I sent an email to Kevin and Lou about this credit, and got a reply from Kevin saying "Already on it." I didn't need that information in the end, but having it filled me with confidence during my ask. After that movie, I received coproducer credit for three more movies—*Iron Man 2*, *Thor*, and *Captain America: The First Avenger*—and was then given executive producer credit with *The Avengers* in 2012 and never looked back.

❧ ❧ ❧

As the years passed and I reached decision-making positions in my career, I set out to use my voice to become a better leader, to advocate for my team, and to fight for them the way no one fought for me. Interestingly, when more women joined us, they brought to light new issues that needed to be addressed. I started hearing many of them fret about having to choose between having a baby and having a career. I connected with them, and then I set out to find a solution. We provided new mothers with the possibility to choose whether they preferred to be at the office or work remotely near their baby's nursery at home. We made sure these two roads could coexist. Granted, if you're a cameraperson or actor, for example, it's a different story, because then you need to be on set to carry out your job, so there are exceptions, as there are with every system in place. But if being on set isn't a requirement for the job, then where you do the work can be flexible, so long as you can connect and get the job done. Just having the possibility to choose without fearing they might lose their jobs made an enormous difference in employees' lives. It removed a heavy load of stress, and this, in turn, elevated their job performance.

We must consistently aim to be more inclusive. To see things from varying perspectives is incredibly important. It allows us to make movies where more people across the world can begin to identify with the characters and the adversities they face. Different people bring different experiences to the table, and our collective stories become richer and more powerful.

Having a diverse team also gives us a better chance at a fairer degree of representation in our final product. And that will only work if everyone on the team feels safe enough to speak up. I've already shared with you how curiosity feeds my soul. But quiet curiosity doesn't amount to much. So I try to lead through example by asking as many questions as needed to understand what's at stake. One thing to keep in mind is that Hollywood consistently suffers from imposter syndrome. And many people who have every bit of what it takes to be in the room and ask the right questions to get the job done at times let their fears and sense of inadequacy get the best of them. Though I clearly understand that with some positions people may be afraid to ask questions of those in power or perceived power, I constantly strive to create a space where my team members can operate from respect rather than fear, where challenging opinions about projects are welcomed and valued.

When I was in the room with my team at Marvel, I'd often say to them, "Tell me why we should or shouldn't do this." "Tell me why you think this is happening and what we can do to make it better." And most important: "What is it that I'm not doing that I could be doing to make it better?" This last question was key to letting my team know that they could speak up and let me know if there was anything I could improve. I dug further by asking, "What can I do?" "How can I do it better?" This set the stage for others on my team to feel comfortable asking questions and raising issues too. "Wait, I'm sorry, why are we doing this?" "Okay, so when you do that, where does it have to go next?" "Oh, is this new?" "Why would this character do that?" That's just a sample of the questions that came from me on any given day in any department at any level at Marvel. My teams were usually pretty hard on me, speaking up and telling me exactly what was on their minds and what we could potentially do to fix any issues we ran into throughout the production process. I respect how vocal they were and appreciate that they felt comfortable enough to express what was on their mind. That's the best way to work. I like to know how things function, and I pride myself on staying on top of any new developments in software, systems, and graphics. The more I know, the more efficient my leadership will be. At the end of the day, I will take every single opinion from any of my teams into consideration.

Asking questions didn't just keep me up to date with how we worked; it connected me to the teams in my departments. Through these conversations, I was able to stay in tune with the people who made the magic happen behind closed doors. So if I know you're more productive at night, I won't ask you to be at the office by eight in the morning. I'll talk to you so we can set a later work schedule to fit you. Why? Because if I push you to come in early when you're naturally not as alert as you could be, then I'm not going to get the best of you to deal with what we have on our plate. I understand that certain companies require a level of structure, but we had the opportunity to do things slightly differently, so why not? As long as we overlapped for a few hours to field questions, I didn't care what shifts the teams chose. This was one of the reasons we had such a tight group of people at Marvel who consistently helped us deliver the impossible. Once you reach a position of power, honor what your team needs to succeed. It's not about you; it's about your people, the collective striving for the same goal.

Throughout the years, I have made it a point to regularly tell the teams what I was doing, and why. I always wanted them to have all the tools at their disposal in case they needed to move a project forward without me. I liked to let them into my process, my thinking, my decision-making. If you work with me, you will always know where I stand. If you don't know, it's because I haven't figured it out yet either. I have always *chosen* to be transparent, even when I realized that if I would've kept my mouth shut and not been so opinionated or transparent in this business, I might have gone further up the career ladder sooner. But had I done that, who would I have become?

❮ ❮ ❮

When the coronavirus hit the United States in March 2020 and our government asked us to stay at home, we followed suit and began working remotely, as did most nonessential companies across the country. This brought on a kaleidoscope of terrible and wonderful moments that we had to navigate to the best of our abilities as a team, as a company, and as a country.

Many of the team members had people who passed away, as did I. If you had kids, you were homeschooling, so you had to do that extra job on top of your own. The kids went through terrible withdrawals, and I think it has affected that generation in ways we are yet to discover. We were all worried about the physical and mental health toll those weeks and then months would have on them and us. Yet, amid the ailments and rising number of deaths that shriveled our hearts, we had to figure out how to operate remotely and keep folks employed.

And so began the endless Zoom meetings with their now classic phrases: "You're muted," "Your camera is off," "Please mute yourself." This shift in how we operated also opened a window into each of our homes. We got to meet one another's children as they inevitably peered over our shoulders or popped up in the background while we were looking at postproduction imagery. And then there were the pets, who made us chuckle with their resounding meows or incessant barks demanding the door be opened and who warmed our hearts with their on-camera presence. On my end, I was pet-sitting my kid's godparents' dog, Oliver. During the first three or four days, he had major anxiety and his howls seeped into every one of my daily meetings. Then by day four, he stopped. Meanwhile, my mom, who lived with us during that time, didn't quite grasp that our meetings involved a camera, so she'd walk into the room and talk to me as if I was alone. A couple of times, while I was taking part in a panel with 1,500 people watching, my mom walked in and loudly asked me about the bathroom and where I'd left the towels. As stressful as those awkward situations were, they also provided comic relief at a moment in time when we had no clue what to expect next.

As for the work, well, we didn't know how to produce remotely because we'd never before had to do this. What's more, we had people stuck across the world who had been on location when the lockdown domino effect came, and we had to figure out how to bring them home safely as soon as possible. That itself became its own crusade because every part of the world was affected at a slightly different time. *Chaos* doesn't even begin to cover it. I think it was probably one of the most stressful times of my entire career. There we were, a bunch of type A control freaks at the helm of something no one could control, especially at the beginning when we didn't know anything about covid-19. And as production people, who are used to finding the source of the issue and doing whatever is needed to solve it, the not knowing drove us up the wall.

With the passing days, we did our best to adjust to working remotely amid the palpable fear of the unknown. Things failed on the regular. In production, we're used to obstacles, but these were completely new to us because they were happening in our homes. There were connectivity issues and endless distractions, not just from our families and pets, but also from deliveries at the door, neighbors playing music or mowing their lawns, sounds that bled into our meetings, all things that were out of our control. We also lost that personal touch that comes with running into someone in an elevator, walking to get a cup of coffee, or sharing a chat in the hallway. Those moments that allowed for us to check in on one another basically vanished as we jumped from one online meeting to the next. Suddenly, we found ourselves sitting at our desks for twelve to fourteen hours a day without the respite that comes with a walk from one building to the next. It became quite robotic, almost like a game of resilience. After a while, I learned to build in time between Zooms to stretch my legs or grab a glass of water, but for many of us it was mayhem, one of the greatest exercises of patience of our lives—especially when you're used to a certain speed and efficiency. Yet somehow, we got through it and managed to keep the Marvel ship afloat.

The first week we were allowed to return to the studio, I remember waiting in my car for my turn to pass through Disney's security gate, and as I approached the entrance, one of my favorite guards said, "I'm so sorry you had to wait, Ms. Alonso."

"Are you kidding me?" I replied ecstatically. "I'm just so happy we're back!" I looked at him and we both smiled widely, knowing that this moment meant so much more than just waiting in line at the gate.

Tears filled my eyes as I drove through those gates. It was an incredibly emotional week for everyone. We were still masked up and keeping our distance, so although we were finally able to stand in the same rooms together, we couldn't hug one another or share smiles. But there was a kinetic vibe in the air, filled with hope that we might slowly be inching to the other side of this devastating pandemic. During this time, despite all odds, we managed to create beautiful work—like the show *WandaVision* as well as other TV series, which were a first for many of us at the studio. We also started an animation branch at the studio, something we'd never done before either. In a way, having to suddenly shut down productions and put release dates on hold was a blessing. It allowed us to think about our current projects without delivery dates siphoning our attention. We finished many and then shelved them until further notice. This pivot also opened the door to working remotely one or two days a week. I used to spend many of my weekends at the office, but this time allowed me to recenter my priorities and only do so when something urgent needed attention. Anything else could now be taken care of on Zoom. Ultimately, from the devastation came a better way of living and working.

❝ ❝ ❝

When we begin to hold positions of power, we have the possibility to stand up for what's right on a bigger scale, and we mustn't take that for granted. Our voices can now be used not just to advocate for ourselves and our teams but for the larger good.

When I'm in the presence of someone who makes a passing remark or joke that I believe to be offensive, I don't just sit there and look the other way. I speak up in a respectful manner and express my discomfort. No matter how small the utterance may seem, if we don't speak up, we are quietly allowing those comments to become accepted in conversation—another example of why silence can be poison.

Instead of forcing a laugh and hoping the person takes the hint and changes the subject, why not just say, for example, "Please don't say that joke about gay people. You don't realize how hurtful those jokes are." If enough people raise their voices, those jokes will soon be a thing of the past.

❮ ❮ ❮

The first time I decided to go out with a woman, I didn't hide it. I raised my voice and openly mentioned it to my mom during one of our phone calls.

"I'm going on a date with a girl."

"What do you mean, a date?" she asked.

"A date," I said.

"Like a date, date?" she probed.

"Yes, a date, date."

"Oh."

My message was clear: You can either be a part of my life during whatever I go through, or not. She took her time to digest this news. By no means did this change of heart signify that my first marriage was anything but real. It wasn't like I loved women all my life and kept it a secret to hide my real sexuality. No, I loved my husband. My heart was heavy when our marriage ended. I didn't really consider dating women until the possibility presented itself, and the first thing I thought was *Why not?*

Soon after our talk, my mom suffered a small stroke and had to undergo an angioplasty. I traveled to Argentina to be by her side. And after she recovered and we were left alone in her room, she finally said, "Well, I want you to know that I don't understand why you choose to be with women. To me, it's as if you are telling me you want to be a nun. You were never into religion, never wore nunlike clothes, didn't pray, didn't hang out with people from the Church. And suddenly, now you're in your late twenties and you're telling me you want to devote your life to the Church? Being gay is a foreign concept to me, but I talked to my priest, to my therapist, to my healer, and I've done a lot of work about your decision, so if you go back to men, I'll kill you."

I was direct and honest with her, and I also understood that she had needed a little time to catch up to what I knew to be true in my heart. She never said she outright accepted my being gay—to this day, I don't think she has, and I believe she'd give anything for me to go back to men—but she's learned to live with it because she chose to continue having me in her life.

Coming out wasn't a struggle for me, and I always make sure to clarify this when the subject comes up. People sometimes mirror your shame with their lack of acceptance. Because if you're ashamed of who you are, then there must be something wrong with you, which is how the nonaccepter feels, so you're validating that person's feelings. The more we are able to share our experiences, whether they were a struggle or not, without shades of shame, the more people will accept our love stories and finally understand that our choices do not threaten their way of life. Love is love.

❦ ❦ ❦

I wish I could say the only times I have had to speak up for my LGBTQIA+ community were to quell disrespectful jokes, but then came March 8, 2022, when Florida approved its "Don't Say Gay" bill, which regulates lessons and limits discussions on gender identity and sexual orientation in classrooms across the state. The sheer disappointment sliced off a piece of my heart. And a few weeks later, while accepting a GLAAD Media Award for Outstanding Film for *Eternals,* I couldn't help but use that mic to voice my concerns publicly:

> *If you are a member of the LGBTQIA community and you work at the Walt Disney Company, the last two or three weeks have been a sad event. I've asked Mr. Chapek for courage. In a forty-five-minute sit-down I asked him to look around and truly, if what we sell is entertainment for the family, that we don't choose what family. Family is this entire room. Family is the family in Texas, in Arizona, in Florida, and in my family, in my home. So I ask you again, Mr. Chapek, please respect—if we're selling family—take a stand against all of these crazy outdated laws. Take a stand for family. Stop saying that you tolerate us—nobody tolerates me, let me tell you that. You*

tolerate the heat in Florida, the humidity in Arizona
or Florida, and the dryness in Arizona and Texas.
And you tolerate a tantrum in a two-year-old. But you
don't tolerate us. We deserve the right to live, love,
and have. More importantly, we deserve an origin
story. . . . I encourage all of you to stop being silent.
Silence is death . . . silence is poison. . . . Fight, fight,
fight. As long as I'm at Marvel Studios, I will fight for
representation. I see you.

An emotional plea felt right in that moment. It came from a place of love. I had done press for *Eternals,* but I hadn't attended that event with this intention. The possibility presented itself, and I said yes.

Your voice will not only help you; it also has the power to give other people a voice and make an impact on their lives.

If silence is poison, our voice is the antidote. Ask for what you think you deserve at work and in your relationships, stay curious, and when you finally have a spot at the table, use it to speak up and stand up for what you believe. As the American psychiatrist David Viscott once said, "The purpose of life is to discover your gift. The work of life is to develop it. The meaning of life is to give your gift away."

My gift is my voice. What's yours?

9

Be Humble

"Silence your ego and your power will rise."

—THE ANCIENT ONE, *DOCTOR STRANGE* (2016)

There's a corner store down the road from my home that has two words painted on its sprawling exterior wall: BE HUMBLE. The first time I pointed it out to my kid, she was rather young and could barely read, but I taught her to spell the words, and every time we'd drive by that wall we'd talk about what those two words meant. I was fascinated time and again by what humility was in my child's eyes. Way too many people lose sight of their humility once they attain great success; however, being and remaining humble is an integral part of the foundation of what we've set out to build within my family. If you don't stay humble, everything you've worked so hard to accomplish on a personal and professional level will crumble. Why? Because the ego is the cousin no one wants to invite to the family gathering. The one who has lost perspective and believes life revolves around them.

In *Thor*, when Thor defies his father's wishes and travels to Jotunheim to confront the Frost Giants for attempting to retrieve a source of power, called the Casket of Ancient Winters, from Asgard, a battle unfolds, breaking a long-running yet fragile truce between the two planets. Ultimately, Thor's father, Odin, must step in to rescue Thor and those who have followed him on this calamitous mission. Back home, Thor and Odin erupt into a war of words. Thor impulsively defends his actions: "There won't be a kingdom to protect if you're afraid to act. The Jotuns must learn to fear me, just as they once feared you." Disappointed, Odin replies, "That's pride and vanity talking, not leadership." After another heated exchange, Odin grows quiet and realizes his son is not ready to assume his role as Asgard's king. Instead, he decides to banish his son to Earth, stripping him of his hammer and powers to teach him a lesson. Thor must learn how to set his ego aside and become humble to be worthy of regaining his power. And he does so when he redirects his strength for the good of humankind.

❮ ❮ ❮

When people ask me, "What is power? What is success?" I start off by explaining that my idea of success is different from many other people's perception of this concept. I feel successful when I am able to get through the day in the healthiest and most joyful way possible. I see my work as a gift, a chance to tell stories, a privilege, but no matter how far I climb up the proverbial ladder, I never feel like I've arrived. The feeling of arrival, of making it, becomes palpable to me when I hear someone say to me, "I never even considered the possibility of this career path, but when I saw your name in the credits and realized you're like me—Latina, gay, immigrant—I realized that if you could do it, there's a chance I could too." Paving the way for all people to be at the table, opening those doors, creating accessible possibilities for future generations regardless of their backgrounds, leaving that legacy—that is my definition of success. I would rather be a good person than a successful one.

At the end of the day, it's not just about you or me—it's about the collective. The different perspectives of every member of our team helped us hold one another accountable. We constantly challenged each other during the making of our films and shows. "Wait, why would he do that?" one of them would say of a character. "Hmm, I don't think she'd say such a thing," I would add. When we set aside our egos and remained receptive to this type of open and honest dialogue, we were able to create more sparks of creativity and open the floor to new ideas from the rest of the people in the room.

This is the model I liked to use with all our teams. I don't believe in a pyramid type of hierarchy at work—I know some may find this useful, and it may even be necessary for certain businesses, but *my way or the highway* is the opposite of how I function. I never want to feel like I'm above anyone else, and I'm not interested in a fight between egos. I'm interested in great storytelling, and that's achieved when we work side by side and as a team. I see the people I work with more as forming a fluid bubble, in constant motion, joining forces so that we make it to the finish line without popping. Sure, the bubble may temporarily shift into a pyramid if I have to make a final call, but by and large, I want us to roll with it together. Within this fluid bubble, I continuously encourage my teams to speak up and give it to me straight. What's more, not listening to people just because on paper they may not have as much experience as the old guard makes no sense to me either. Some of the best advice I've received has actually come from those who are new to the industry because they have a fresh take that may lead to a marvelous solution none of us have thought of before. These interactions give me life. They create new possibilities.

I thrive on change—that's why I'm so enamored by storytelling from the point of view of technology and visual effects, because it is constantly evolving. Just when you think you have a good grasp on how it works and what it can do, a new feature changes the game all over again. It keeps us on our toes, that's for sure, and it also keeps us humble. This reminds me of a poster I had on my bedroom wall as a young girl, the last memory I have of my room before I moved to the United States: a gorilla with a quizzical expression looking into the camera, with a caption that read: JUST WHEN I LEARNED ALL THE ANSWERS, THEY CHANGED ALL THE QUESTIONS. That phrase remained vividly in my mind as I navigated my career in Hollywood. It's filmmaking in a nutshell. You learn as you go. Many of today's answers will likely be different from the ones we will arrive at a year from now.

❰ ❰ ❰

If you walk into this industry with too much cockiness, Hollywood will eventually show you who's the boss. Because in this town you may be the cream of the crop one day and forgotten the next. That's why it's important that you stay humble. This is an unpredictable business. I used to consistently tell younger generations at Marvel Studios, "I will work for you one day." Because I've seen it happen. I've worked for people at the start of my career who later worked on my team. That's why one of my anchors to professional humility is reminding myself daily that the work I do is a privilege, and it is temporary. At some point in my career my time will be over too, and it will be somebody else's turn to rise to the top. So I don't buy into that "I'm irreplaceable" messaging. This attitude helps keep my humility alive and my cocky Argentinian side under wraps.

Instead of acting like you're owed a certain respect because of your position or title, appreciate each moment and focus on equally respecting everyone who crosses your path, no matter where they fall in your industry's hierarchy. I make a point of focusing on the human behind the title. When I was at Marvel, I didn't talk to the prop master or the special effects supervisor: I talked to the people who happened to have these titles. Because I knew who they were; I had known them for a long time. When I saw someone on my team struggling, I asked them how their family was doing, how they were doing. Making that connection turned that worker into a person. We all struggle. We all have good and bad days. We all have moments when things are developing at home that don't allow us to focus the same way at work, regardless of the title we hold. And that's okay. The beauty of working as a team is that when someone has to take a step back, someone else is willing to take a step forward to fill in that gap.

So next time you're interacting with someone on the job, set aside your title, your career, your power, and remember that the boss, coworker, team member, or employee in front of you is simply another human being. I talk to a CEO the same way I talk to a valet or to the person who cleaned the second floor of the Frank G. Wells Building at Marvel. I talk to a highly regarded director the same way I talk to a production assistant. Our accomplishments will not disappear if we're the ones getting the coffee for another person for a change or if we have to park farther away because our regular spot is taken. The minute you forget about the humanity of your coworkers, your humility becomes nonexistent. When on the brink of crossing that disjointed line, remember this to ground yourself: We are all just a bunch of flawed humans trying to figure out how to best navigate this thing called life. At the end of the day, it really is that simple.

Another key humility anchor I use to keep me grounded is nurturing the connections with people beyond Hollywood, beyond work, with those who have known me before all of this. I do have a few friends in the industry too, but they're usually not the ones I go to the movies with or call at night when I need to talk something out on a personal level. Those conversations are left for my longtime friends, like Alejo and Elena, who are like my brother and sister. They've known me since I was a kid. And they will set me straight in the blink of an eye when needed.

Surround yourself with people who will tell it like it is and won't *yes* their way through your life. And, as my friend Bonnie Curtis—a film producer who worked with Steven Spielberg for a long time—recommends, "Answer every phone call. Get back to people. It doesn't matter if it takes you a month. Call them back." That is one of the pieces of advice I live by. I do my best to carry this out with conviction, and if I can't call someone back, I find someone who will guide them with what they need. In Hollywood, people go through cycles: One day you are at a high level of success and the next day you might be out of a job—but talented people tend to bounce back and find their way. So call people back regardless of where they are in their own "success cycle."

❝ ❝ ❝

Another tool I use to help keep myself in check—which I like to practice on a regular basis and which I hope you too will incorporate into your life regardless of what you do for work—is the Make Three Phone Calls exercise. These calls are gifts that we can give and receive today. They're within our reach. They're phone calls that I have made and continue to make on a regular basis to maintain harmony in my life.

First, make a call for yourself that you have been putting off. You know, the one you've been wanting to make to move yourself forward on a personal or professional level, where you ask for something you want or deserve. If you don't ask, it will never happen. Do it. Give yourself that gift. You're worth it. The potential gain is huge, and the loss is nil if it's a dead-end street. Remember, you essentially already have a no by not asking for it.

Next, make a call exclusively for someone else, with no strings attached. Don't just be humble—be kind, and do this for someone just because you can. You have no idea how much you can change someone's life with one short phone call. No matter where you are in your career, whether you're a page, an assistant, a producer, or a president, this type of help and kindness is within your power. Put it to good use.

I made one such call recently for an actor turned director. She was talking to me about her project during lunch one day when I noticed her usual effervescence was suddenly clouded with worry.

"What's going on?" I asked.

"Well, I know the studio is into it, but I think they're having doubts about moving forward because I'm a first-time director."

"I'll call her," I said, referring to the person making the decisions for this project.

"Why? You don't even know if I can do it."

"No, but I think I do. I think you'll be fine. And if you get in a bind and it all goes to hell, call me. I'll help you."

Sometimes a capable person just needs another capable person to give them a vote of confidence. Later that afternoon, I picked up the phone and made the call.

"I believe in her," I said. "I believe in her dedication, I believe she has the eye for the job, I believe in who she is, and if she's ever in need, I will help her."

I honestly don't think my call got her project off the ground, because, from what I gathered, it was already in the bag, but maybe it helped clear any lingering doubt in this person's mind.

I've made thousands of calls like this. And I've never received that call asking me to take over a project, because the people I vouched for have never failed. The fact that someone believes in you as a filmmaker is huge. And to the person taking the risk and hiring you, knowing that another capable person believes in you and has offered an open phone line to help you become a stronger filmmaker is important too.

Sometimes this call for someone else simply comes down to a few words of encouragement to help them set aside any hint of doubt. Other times, this call may be about getting their foot in the door or a job offer. Many people do not know how to access this industry, how to get in, but with a little push in the right direction, they may have what it takes to jump-start a career they didn't even realize they could have. I've made calls that have led me to hire people with all types of work backgrounds, from a parking valet to a Starbucks barista. If I see they have a producer's mind-set or have the potential to become producers, then I will give them a shot. You can learn the history of film in your spare time, but the instincts of a producer are hard to teach. It's amazing how one short call might be the key to a big shift in someone else's life. Don't underestimate your power to make a difference.

The third call in this exercise is aimed at helping you turn resentment into forgiveness. Yes, I left the hardest one for last, but it's one of the most healing moments you may ever experience. Oftentimes, resentment is a one-way street. You may be upset with a friend, colleague, or family member, harboring this ill feeling within you. And they may be none the wiser because you've never talked to them directly about what's bothering you. If you live with resentment, churning the pain in your mind as you break down every last second of what led you to feel this in the first place, you are unconsciously creating your own hurdle surrounded by an all-consuming negative energy field. And as that negative energy grows, it takes up space that should have been allotted for the positive things heading your way. The only one at the losing end of this stick is you, if you don't speak up.

Start by digging in a little deeper to get to the root of this resentment. Talk about it with yourself before you reach out to the people or structure that created this feeling within you. Turn resentment into forgiveness by forgiving yourself first. Figure out your role in the event in question and forgive yourself for any mistakes you may have made.

If the situation or issue at stake truly has no solution—if it involves someone with whom you will not be able to talk to under any circumstances or an issue on a film or project you cannot fix no matter how hard you've tried—then focus on forgiving yourself, work on slowly letting the issue and resentment go, and do your best to move on. In the process, allow yourself to say "Well, that was not a win, and that's okay." Give yourself a break. No matter how many accomplishments you may have to your name, we all have limitations, doubts, struggles, and failures. So put that feeling of dejection and resentment in a balloon and let it float up into the sky and expand until it explodes. Then say goodbye—what's done is done. By forgiving yourself and releasing that resentment, you are actively creating space for love and joy and new possibilities. Now, as you move forward, continue to give your best to all you do, regardless of whether your best will get the results you hope for.

In my opinion, making *Black Panther* was difficult not just in size and scale but because of the meaning it carried—what it could potentially represent for Black and brown people was gigantic—so the responsibility we all carried on our shoulders was massive. During this time, I had several conversations with first-time production designer Hannah Beachler. The enormity of it all often became overwhelming to her, but I continuously reassured her that she was the right person for the job and often said, "Repeat this to yourself: *I did my best, and my best was good enough.*" I found that line so powerful that I would often email or text it to her as a reminder. Several months later, Hannah walked onstage to receive her Academy Award for Best Production Design for *Black Panther,* and at the end of her beautiful and stirring speech, she repeated this exact line: "I give this strength to all of those who come next, to keep going, to never give up, and when you think it's impossible, just remember to say this piece of advice I got from a very wise woman: 'I did my best, and my best is good enough.'" We must remind ourselves that we can't resent ourselves for something we didn't do if what we did was the best that we could. Sometimes that's all we have to give in a specific moment in time.

Now, if there are more parties involved, and there's a sliver of possibility to reach out and talk your resentment through with them and turn it into forgiveness, then do not hesitate to make that call. You will likely curse me while you're in the thick of it because it's no walk-in-the-park-on-a-sunny-day kind of chat, but you will be grateful later. It is one of the hardest and oftentimes one of the best phone calls you will ever make. As you enter the conversation, do your best, without pointing any fingers, to clearly explain how what happened affected you. Stay calm. In an ideal world, you will have the opportunity to talk it out, clarify any misunderstandings, forgive, and move on, but we don't live in an ideal world. Therefore, that call cannot come from a desire to hear the other person say "I'm sorry." Some people will think there's nothing to be forgiven and don't even consider your concern as an issue. This call should stem from your own need for closure. It is ultimately for you to say your piece so that you can forgive and move on. The outcome is *you* making the phone call. Not the outcome of the phone call itself.

A musician friend of mine used that phone call with the producer who did her previous album, someone she resented but with time realized had been one of her best producers. When she called and asked if they could get past their differences, that person said, "Of course, I got past that months ago." That resentment wasn't living in him; it was only living in her. And that one call cleared the path for forgiveness and created space for either a possible new beginning between them, or at the very least a sense of closure.

If you can't bring yourself to make this call, it's okay. Don't beat yourself up over that. Instead, maybe try to write it all down in a letter and then either send it or trash it or burn it. The whole point of this forgiveness practice is to depart that island of resentment on the forgiveness boat and get back to a place of love. Yesterday has passed, tomorrow is yet to come, but today is *everything*.

❮ ❮ ❮

I always sense the second hand of a clock ticking over my head, marking the passage of time. And this pushes me to question myself on a daily basis: *Am I making the right choice in how I spend my time? Have I done enough? Have I given enough? Am I leaving this place better than I found it?* Since my dad died when he was forty years old, each year I have on him feels like a gift. As I write this, I am seventeen years older than he was when he passed away, but will I make it to eighteen? I don't know—no one does. Am I winning the battle against time? No. Never. That is one battle none of us will win. But at least I know in my heart I am giving it one hell of a fight. This awareness of how short life can be is what inspires me to inject fun into each day, sing, laugh, share, and always voice what needs to be said in case I'm not around to speak my truth tomorrow. Life, just having the privilege to be alive, is one of the main elements that keeps me humble and grounded.

At the end of the day, if you focus solely on the mountain you are building, you risk living in the shadow of that mountain rather than the humbling light found at its summit. As Shuri says in *Black Panther*, "Just because something works doesn't mean it can't be improved." That goes for what we do and who we are too. I refuse to drink the Kool-Aid of my own power because, if I did, then I would no longer be able to live in the world of possibility. Ultimately, it all comes down to harnessing your possibility superpower to go after your dreams, while staying within the light of humility and gratitude every step of the way. There lies the privilege.

10

Choose Love

Thor: "You seek love."
Gorr: "Love? Why should I seek love?"
Thor: "Because it's all any of us want."

—THOR: LOVE AND THUNDER (2022)

The last few years have been riddled with loss and moments of deep reflection that have inspired many of us to pivot and realign ourselves on our path. Covid-19 brought us all together under the same pandemic roof, a place where we were suddenly plunged into grieving the loss of loved ones, the loss of precious time, the loss of freedom to move around, the loss of human touch. But, as Vision says in *WandaVision*, "What is grief, if not love persevering?" In that togetherness, we were able to see what was working and what wasn't, both in our personal and professional lives. Some decided to put in the work to improve what was lacking; others realized no amount of work would fix their situation, so they decided to leave and give themselves a chance to start over; and a few walked away and came back to give it another shot. If anything, this pandemic has been the greatest destabilizer and the great equalizer. It made us stop, face our realities, and summon the courage and honesty to determine what we want and need out of life and in terms of love.

Love—a seemingly small, four-letter word, yet it carries so much weight and importance in our lives. Ultimately, like Thor says to Gorr, the villain of *Thor: Love and Thunder*, love is all any of us want. But that doesn't mean it comes easily to us. We all desire to have love, give love, feel love. And because of this, a lack of love can create one of the deepest craters we face in our journeys. Think about Loki's poignant response when trying to define the meaning of love: "Love is a dagger. It's a weapon to be wielded far away or up close. You can see yourself in it. It's beautiful. Until it makes you bleed." In Loki's unintentional search for love, he found pain and abandonment, which fed his insecurities throughout his life, leading him to wonder if he was ever truly loved by his family. Yet when he finds himself trapped in a time loop cell with Lady Sif, who repeatedly slaps him across the face and says, "I hope you know you deserve to be alone, and you always will be," something shifts within him. After fervently believing he was better off on his own, he realizes he doesn't necessarily want to be alone, especially after meeting Sylvie, his soon-to-be love interest.

Everyone deserves a chance to love and be loved.

But what is love?

Oftentimes, the first thing that comes to mind when we think about love, other than a romantic partner, is family. So, let's start there.

What is family to you?

If you feel your blood relatives are your one and only family, then more power to you. But being born into a specific nucleus of people doesn't mean that we will automatically fit in and get along with them. As we grow up, our individual experiences begin to shape us and set us on our own unique path. And sometimes, that path we take has us looking at life from a fresh perspective, which may not always coincide with that of our family. With time, we may discover we no longer share the same tastes or the same values. Who you consider in your heart of hearts to be family doesn't always have to be those who brought you into the world and share your DNA.

Coming to this realization is no easy endeavor. Our individual growth and evolution don't mean we love our biological family any less, but we may not always like them. This, in turn, is what drives us to create our own pod, a place where we feel safe and loved without judgment, our chosen family.

That chosen family theme is found in most, if not all, of the MCU films I worked on. Whether it's the Guardians of the Galaxy, Captain Marvel, Black Widow, or the Avengers in their search for their identities, most of our characters find the support and love that fuels their strength from their core group of people, and these people are usually not defined by bloodlines. They choose to have such people in their lives, to rely on them, because they make their hearts sing and provide them with a sense of comfort and unconditional love. Take Natasha Romanoff—by the end of

Black Widow she and her sister, Yelena, realize that despite not being born of the same parents, they have an undeniable sibling bond. What's more, Natasha works out her childhood issues and comes to terms with the fact that she doesn't have one family but two, and neither are her blood relatives.

❦ ❦ ❦

Sometimes our friends are our family. Sometimes our partner or our pets are our family. There is no formula for how to create a family. I will always love my mom and my sister, but I have also come to accept that our roads have forked into very different paths, which we may not understand all the time, but which we accept. And so, throughout my more than five decades of life on Earth, like many of our superheroes, I have sought out my own chosen families too. From Alejo García Pintos, a childhood friend whom I consider my brother, to my colleagues with whom I'm in the trenches day in and day out. They have all been a steady force in my life, my place of stability, support, and happiness—in many ways, my home. And then came my ultimate chosen family member: my daughter.

I always wanted to have children, but I never had the need to experience maternity from the womb—though I completely respect women who do. My dream was to give a child in need of a home a safe place to grow up, surrounded by love and support. I explored the idea of having kids in my first marriage, but I felt the timing was off. Thankfully, in my second marriage, our paths and desires aligned on this front, which is why on December 23, 2009, the day after my birthday, my wife and I decided to start down the road to adoption. Seven months later, we were holding Raven in our arms. She was the missing piece in our lives.

When Raven was around four years old, she was playing with her toys when she suddenly stopped, turned to us, and said, "Thank you for adopting me." Tears blurred our eyes. When I heard those words come out of that small human being, the world seemed right. That was certainly one of the most profound moments of my life.

In addition to creating a net of love for Raven, the one thing we consistently tell her is "Your voice matters. Always. Not only in the house but outside the house." She has always been an opinionated little one, much like my superhero Mafalda. But as the years went on and the opinions kept coming, I would jokingly say, "Raven, I want you to have an opinion, but not in this house."

She would look at me for a brief second, then crack a big smile and reply, "That's very funny."

She has done that since she was around three years old. That's when I knew she was going to be fine as a kid. She has been empowered to have a voice and speak her mind. We also make sure to infuse her with the power of possibility every chance we get. The messaging is clear: There's nothing you can't do. You just have to get out there and work really hard to achieve your goals.

❮ ❮ ❮

No matter our age or our circumstances, we all need a net of love to catch us when we fall. That net is the emotional support we seek throughout our lives. Sometimes it comes from our colleagues, friends, and family, and other times it comes from sports or music or a pint of ice cream. The net could also be cast by a person who happens to be in your life in that fleeting moment. There are those who are with us for the long haul and others who pass through our lives during brief seasons, yet they all have a meaningful purpose. It's up to us to accept these energies as little saving graces; they will help us get back on our feet and take the next steps forward.

"But in times of crisis the wise build bridges, while the foolish build barriers. We must find a way to look after one another." Those words spoken by T'Challa in *Black Panther* struck a deep chord in me. I believe in the human spirit. Happiness is not right or left leaning. Neither is guilt, deception, integrity, or love. They are universal human values, traits, and emotions that are present in every nook and cranny of the world. Nonacceptance and rejection usually stem from fear of the unknown. Oftentimes, the unknown has been marginalized and hidden, but that doesn't mean it doesn't exist. There isn't an LGBTQIA+ cave where we all hide out. We exist in society. We come from similar families and create our own families. We're your friends, your cousins, your neighbors, your coworkers. My family is not a threat to your way of life. And you'd probably realize this if you only took the time to get to know us.

I believe we can get out of any crisis if we learn how to communicate from the heart, with love, regardless of our similarities or differences. Real communication entails meeting each other halfway, in the middle of a bridge, and having an open, honest, and respectful dialogue. Communicating isn't just talking; it's listening. We need to keep a clear mindset, stay humble with our beliefs, and remain open to understanding other perspectives. That is one of the essential keys to long-lasting progress.

I've always aimed to create art that reflects today's society. During my time at Marvel we pushed boundaries, and we might have ruffled a few feathers along the way, but we were also opening people's eyes to realities they might not have completely understood or accepted until then. And if they still don't understand and accept those realities through those films, at the very least they've had some exposure to another point of view, which is an enormous stride forward. So please consider a powerful African royal family. Please consider Carol Danvers in charge. I keep coming back to *Black Panther* and *Captain Marvel* because they are the pillars of the building I hope to leave as my legacy as a storyteller and a filmmaker. Those two films were a leap of faith toward the "unproven formulas" and have helped to pave the way for so many more to come.

A while back, I got an email from a guy in his late twenties.

> *I don't know you, but I want to share this with you. My father and I hadn't spoken for ten years. He called me one day out of the blue and said, 'I want to go see this superhero movie with you because I know you love them.' Since I liked superhero movies, I said yes to my father, a man I do not love, a man I didn't have a word with for a decade. I went, sat there for two hours, and laughed and cried, as did he. So I thought, why can't*

I love this man if we feel the same and we think the same way? Thank you for bringing us closer. Even if it was for those two hours....

The fact that this man was able to find a common, healing ground with his father, even if only for a couple of hours, filled me with immense satisfaction and gratitude as a filmmaker. In telling stories, I wish to move you, to make you feel something, and to inspire you to build those bridges toward the people you are distanced from, to share common ground with others, and to sit in the discomfort of a new idea—as well as to simply entertain you.

❦ ❦ ❦

I talk to everybody, and I will always be open to meeting with a fellow rebel, speaking with that person, breaking bread with them. Because if we don't stir up some dust, change will remain out of reach. That's why, in 2019, when Gustavo Silva, La Plata's then secretary of culture, and my friend Alejo presented me with the possibility to meet Pope Francis, I said yes. I consider myself a spiritual person, but I'm not religious. Yes, I have been baptized, and I've had my First Holy Communion and have been confirmed in the Catholic Church, but I do not feel aligned with any religious institutions. I find it mind-boggling when nonacceptance is driven by religion, because I believe God loves us all. God is Love. I align with all who believe this essential premise. Nevertheless, I welcomed the opportunity to sit down with the pope, even though we held many differing opinions. Open, honest, respectful

communication between contrasting perspectives can be the catalyst for change. As Yusuf Khan says in *Ms. Marvel*, "A man has
one fundamental choice in life. To live a life in fear or love. A man
who chooses love chooses joonoon, passion. He chooses faith,
courage."

I flew to Rome in January 2022. I had been there a couple of
months earlier for the world premiere of *Eternals*, with the most
diverse cast in MCU history. The city had opened a roped-off
section of its magnificent Colosseum just for us, and we had two
hundred drones equipped with LEDs spell out the word *Eternals*
up above the ancient amphitheater. As we looked to the sky, the
crisp air was imbued with magic and, for a brief moment, a sense
of peace and hope reigned supreme. I had tried to schedule the
meeting with Pope Francis to coincide with this visit, but his cal-
endar was full, which was what brought me back to the Eternal
City at the start of 2022.

On the evening of my arrival, I had a private meeting with
Monsignor Lucio Adrian Ruiz, the secretary of the Vatican
Dicastery for Communication, also a fellow Argentinian, from
Santa Fe. The goal was to coach me on protocol and what to say
during my meeting with the pope. I didn't have an agenda. I was
walking into this experience with the utmost respect and an open
mind. I would've liked to bring my wife with me to meet him so
that he could see us as a couple, but due to covid-19 restrictions
only one person was allowed at a time.

The following afternoon, I headed over to Casa Santa Marta,
a building that stands next to St. Peter's Basilica in Vatican City,
which functions as a guesthouse for visiting clergy and has been

home to Pope Francis since 2013. (He opted to live in a suite in this building rather than the papal apartments in the Apostolic Palace.) I was his last meeting of the day.

I approached the main entrance, which was flanked by Swiss guards dressed in their yellow-, blue-, and red-striped uniforms, nodded at them, and walked in. I was then led into a room with cream-colored walls and a tan-colored sofa and matching arm-chairs and was told the pope would join me shortly. As I stood there and looked around the sparsely decorated space, I couldn't help but recall the last time I came face-to-face with this religious institution.

I was fourteen. My mom and I were attending Sunday mass at our local church. The priest was in the middle of his sermon when suddenly he stated, "Women were made to have children and reproduce." According to this man, that was our ultimate duty, to get married and procreate. Unable to sit quietly with this declara-tion, I stood up and raised my voice from the pews.

"How do you know?" I asked, forthright.

The churchgoers shifted uncomfortably in their seats while a piercing silence filled the cathedral's nave.

"You're not married," I pushed on. "You don't have a family. You're not a woman."

My mom began to frantically tug at my sleeve, urging me with hushed vehemence to sit down, but I ignored her quiet pleas.

"What if I don't want to have kids? Does that mean God won't love me?"

Stunned by the audacity of this teenage girl who had dared to speak her mind in this sacred religious space, he managed to pivot with a slew of nonanswers. Once I realized what was happening, I sat down with the start of what was to be an enduring sense of disappointment settling in my mind and did my best to *tolerate* the rest of the sermon. When the mass was over, as we walked up the aisle toward the exit, the priest approached my mom and me and said, "If that's the way you choose to behave, then neither of you are welcome here."

"Then I'm not coming back to this church," replied my mother, defiantly. And she kept her word. She found another church and never set foot in that building again. Since then, my visits to cathedrals around the world have been driven by an architectural or historic curiosity, but I never attended mass again.

Standing in Vatican City, more than forty years later, I set aside this memory and looked down at the Mafalda bag I had in my hands, which held a gift for the pope, and read the writing on the side panel: "Lo importante es ser uno mismo" (*Being yourself is all that matters*). That's a code I live by, a banner I hold high as I march along my path. And when I had done my research prior to this day and understood everything Pope Francis had accomplished in his life, I realized that this man had remained true to who he is, despite death threats, despite the papal coronation. This, in turn, evoked the utmost respect from my heart. I was eager to meet this man of principle with the rebellious spirit.

When Pope Francis walked into the room, I said, "Hi, how are you, Francisco? I come from the other side of the world to visit you. Where would you like to sit?"

"Well, a chair would be good," he replied, cracking a joke from the get-go. I liked that.

As we got comfortable in our respective seats, I gave him the Mafalda bag with a rainbow LED mask inside.

"This will be really fun, because you have your white outfit, and this white mask, and when they least expect it, at the press of a button, you can light it up and get all the colors of the rainbow," I explained as he carefully examined the gift with genuine curiosity.

"I have ideas of what I could do with this," he said, smiling.

"Okay," I replied, "nothing illegal. I don't want to get in trouble."

We continued chitchatting, the jokes kept coming, I sang for him, and the room filled with our incessant laughter.

"What just happened?" the pope said, chuckling. "Nena, you joke around with me, sing two songs, and suddenly I've forgotten all protocol. You've thrown me for a loop, and now I'm talking to you as if we were sitting in the middle of a farm. Nena, you almost got me to curse!"

After breaking the ice with our good cheer, I looked him in the eye and said, "I don't think you know how much young women look up to you and how many of them want to be you." I paused for a second and then continued, "The other day, my daughter asked me if she could be pope someday. And for the first time since she was born, I had to look her in the eye and say no. 'Not because I don't believe you could,' I explained, 'but because there are rules in the Catholic institution, and the rules say that girls can't be pope. But there's a man in the Vatican that I'm going to see soon. He's the pope. Maybe he'll be able to change that for girls around the world. I don't know, I'll ask.'" I took a breath and then added,

"Please tell me, Francisco, if we are all born equal and we are all equal in the eyes of God, why would you deny women around the world the chance to be you?"

He looked at me, glanced down at his lap, took a beat, and then said, "I learn a lot from listening."

This hit home. I could feel a shift in him, but I didn't know how this could affect anything in the future.

"You and I have opposing views on many issues," I said to Pope Francis, "but we both want the world to be better. And we both try to make it better through love, through loving one another. I just thought you should know there are a lot of women that have asked that question, and the Church would be better off by having a female presence in positions of power."

Our conversation that day shifted to many topics. I asked what music he was listening to, and he told me that he hadn't heard anything new in a while. I asked what was stopping him from getting new music, other than being a little "busy," and I reminded him, "Music is food for the soul. Whenever you have a chance, you should get some new music." Since I really didn't have a specific reason to meet with the pope or an ask of him, we just let it flow and enjoyed each other's company. We talked about the Church not accepting gay people, and he reminded me God loves us all. "If you consistently mention that in your speeches, your words would save lives," I said to him. I later mentioned how much abundance there was in Hollywood and how I hated when people threw away food. For the past thirty years, I have encouraged folks to not throw away food at the office or on set and to please take the leftovers home with them. There are a lot of people who don't make enough money and are probably struggling in silence, and taking home some leftovers could help out that week. Some are hesitant at first, but after I explain that if no one took it, the food would be thrown away, most accept.

Pope Francis remained quiet, carefully listening to what I had to share with him, which I quickly noticed was his way. Then he said, "To feed our brothers and sisters is an act of God. You are a lot more Catholic than you think!"

As we were ending our meeting, I said, "Francisco, I'd like you to come over for lunch one day. I'll make you an asado with chorizo and mollejas, and flan with dulce de leche. I'm not asking you to stay long or spend the day, no, no. We can talk for a while, eat, I'll sing you a song, and then you can leave because I am not sure my neighborhood could handle the security circus that follows you around."

"Uy, can you imagine, nena, it could be fun," he replied with a smile. He seemed genuinely touched by the invitation, even though we both knew it would never happen.

When our meeting was over, his bodyguard came in to take the traditional picture.

"Wait, did he smile?" I asked the guard after he snapped the first shot.

"No."

"Francisco, why aren't you smiling? We've been laughing for ninety minutes. And now you're going to give me a sad face?" Then I turned to the bodyguard and said, "Take another picture, please."

The bodyguard looked at the pope, perplexed, and I chimed in again: "Please, don't look at him, that is my phone, so please take another picture." Then I looked at the pope and with a big smile said, "Santo Padre, if you don't smile for me, I won't leave. So you better start smiling."

The second photo caught him giggling at my last audacious round. Then he said, "Vamos, nena, if I don't get you out of here, you won't leave for sure. Come on."

Monsignor Lucio was waiting outside with a box of alfajores for Pope Francis.

"Wow, Lucio. You brought him alfajores and you didn't bring me anything? Not one little gift from Santa Fe," I said, pulling his leg.

Pope Francis jumped in immediately. "No, please, give her my gift."

"Wait a minute, Francisco. That's worse. You're regifting the gift? This is just not right. Are there no good manners out here?"

Pope Francis looked at Monsignor Lucio and said, "Get her out of here now," and we all laughed.

As we were about to leave, he walked over, hugged me, and whispered, "Nena, no dejes de hacer quilombo."

"I promise I won't stop stirring up trouble," I replied, "but you must promise me the same thing."

"I promise," he said.

After our meeting, that same night, someone caught Pope Francis on camera visiting a record store in Rome. A couple of weeks later, I read the following headline: "Pope Francis Urges Parents to 'Never Condemn' Their Gay Children." He said this during his weekly general audience address.

Was this pure coincidence? I don't know. I wouldn't dare think that anything I said fueled these actions. I'm just elated that he did what he did. By saying parents should love their children the way they are, it's likely he prevented some children and teenagers from dying by suicide that week, or maybe he made a few parents think twice before raising their hand and beating their kids into submission, or perhaps he stopped other parents from kicking their offspring out of the house. I know in my heart his words saved lives. He is a rebel at heart and progressive enough to make a difference in his own way, and my soul aligns with that.

Following this enlightening encounter, I received a letter from Pope Francis himself. In it, he thanked me for my visit, messages, and for creating things that inspire people to change for the better. He said he prayed for me and my family and asked me to pray for him. And, with his signature sense of humor, he mentioned a box of empanadas he'd recently received from a restaurant called Qué Quilombo (What a Ruckus) and said that if we ever shared that asado we talked about, it would be a ruckus.

Thank you, Pope Francis. I promise to never lose my sense of humor or my sense of purpose.

❮ ❮ ❮

My heart is at home when I talk to people I agree with on women's rights and human rights and voting rights and reproductive rights. Being on the same page creates a sense of safety. There is no safety when talking to people who have different points of view, but those conversations allow us to learn in leaps and bounds if we remain open to the possibility of conversation.

Talking to someone you like but don't necessarily agree with will always expand your mind. When you do so, try to let your guard down. The act alone of being open to listening to opposing views can be incredibly enriching. Even if you think the conversation went nowhere, at the very least you gave it a shot, you did the best you could, you tried to put yourself in someone else's shoes and see life from their perspective. That's already a huge step toward building bridges. One of the things I think Santiago Mitre, Mariano Llinás, and Martín Mauregui did beautifully with the *Argentina, 1985* script is that they created a political yet nonpartisan story. They didn't turn the lens on the left, right, or center. They didn't focus on a particular party; rather, they zoomed in on human rights that were abused, obliterated, destroyed, and decimated, and told this devastating part of our history from the point of view of a father, a son, a mother, and a daughter, people who could be relatable across the board. The truth is we never know what may come of these difficult and uncomfortable conversations and stories unless we start having and sharing them. We may impact someone's life in ways we can't even imagine, or they may impact ours. As the saying goes, "In our differences lie our strengths," to which I'd like to add: We are not as different as we think we are. Above all else, let love persevere.

11

Know Who
You Are

"At some point, we all have to choose
between what the world wants
you to be and who you are."

—BLACK WIDOW, *BLACK WIDOW* (2021)

In the Marvel movies I worked on, there is always a moment when our heroes will question something about themselves, their life, their choices, their people, their journey—just like us. *Am I on the right path? Is this who I'm supposed to be? Why have I chosen this? Or did it choose me?* Discovering, understanding, and knowing who we are, that's the endgame of every one of our origin stories—it allows us to step into a power that goes beyond any superhero abilities: the power of being our unique, complete, inspiring, beautiful selves.

I have been true to who I am my entire life. I didn't change for my family or friends, I didn't change for my bosses, I didn't change for Hollywood, I didn't change for Marvel, and I didn't change for Disney. I didn't let my industry or anyone else redefine who I am or should be. I chose to never suppress my identity nor code-switch to fit in, because I knew that, at the end of the day, none of that would serve me well. That choice is part of the integrity that I bring to the table; it's part of one of my own superpowers: transparency. And here I am, still standing.

Within your possibilities lies your true identity. You are not Female Alpha Number 2. We're not cookie-cutter beings. We are so much more than that. Like Frigga wisely says to her son Thor, our success is not measured by who we think we're supposed to be but rather who we are.

At some point in our journey, we must stop listening to what people think we should be or do and start paying attention to ourselves and what rings true to each of us as individuals. We have to connect and listen to our instincts. Sure, it's much easier to simply go with the flow and just be who our family, religion, society, partner, or industry wants us to be. The problem arises when what truly makes us happy is replaced by what we've been told should make us happy. Or—to put it another way—when we base our actions on meeting the expectations of those around us while disregarding our own desires and dreams. Do you really want to become a doctor, or do you feel in your heart you would be happier as a writer? Do you really love putting on makeup every day and styling perfectly coiffed hair, or are you just doing it to please your partner? Do you really find your boss's derogatory jokes funny, or are you laughing to appease them? If it feels wrong, it likely is wrong for you.

Oftentimes, people don't listen to their instincts because they're either swayed by someone else's opinion or they live by someone else's compass. It's only natural to latch on to the successful people you admire, to study who they are and what path they took to get there, when you're just starting out. But it's a tricky landscape to traverse because, for the longest time, many of those successful people up top have been straight white men. So, what if you're gay, a person of color, an immigrant, a woman? Many challenges will head your way that can easily veer you in the direction of becoming something the people in this industry want you to be. What's more, Hollywood will not hesitate to mold you into what they need to fit *their* agenda, *their* path, *their* goals. And they won't hesitate to put you on the chopping block when you no longer serve *their* purpose.

I had plenty of opportunities to reject who I was, but instead I doubled down on my identity. When people have found out I'm from Argentina, several conversations have gone down like this:

"But you seem more European."

"No, I'm Argentinian."

"But your last name, wait, what's your heritage?"

"I'm Spanish and Italian."

"See, you're more European."

"No, I'm Argentinian."

I could've taken my European roots for a ride because my

maternal family came from Italy and my paternal side came from Spain, but my two parents are both Argentinian, and I was born and raised in Argentina. I am Argentinian through and through. That means that I'm a Latina, not a European. I chose not to suppress who I was, that's why I corrected them. I never code-switched just to fit in, but I understand dealing with the pressure to belong is so intense that many can't help but succumb to it a little, or a lot. *If I am a little more of what they want me to be, maybe I'll get invited to that meeting, get that promotion, be a part of that team.* That's where it starts. Then you start adjusting your appearance, your way of talking. Sure, you can't hide the color of your skin, but you can straighten your hair, hide your sexuality, and lean on your European roots even though you're from Latin America, all in the name of fitting in and getting ahead. You begin to suppress the parts that you feel won't fly in a certain group, and slowly, somewhere along the way, you risk forgetting who you were to begin with. An identity crisis comes into play and you may not even become aware of it until much later. Then one day, you may look back and think, *Wait, did I get here because of who I am or because I turned into who they wanted me to be?*

Trying to fit in by neglecting your true identity will not help you in the long run because sooner or later the real you will come out, and those around you may interpret your previous actions as disingenuous. Make it a priority to remain connected to you. Don't disappear, don't become a shadow of yourself for a job or for someone else, and don't suppress yourself just to belong. There's a preconceived notion that success must fit a certain pattern. And yes, some jobs require you to take a specific road—you can't become a doctor without going to medical school and completing your residency. But there are other jobs, like my own, where different roads can get you to similar destinations. However, if you don't know who you are, you can easily get lost along the way.

❝ ❝ ❝

You are unique. There is no one else like you in the world. And your unique self is what you should bring to the table. Without that uniqueness, we wouldn't have diversity, and we'd all be the same slices of white bread. Be Hawaiian bread with its signature touch of sweetness. Be rye bread with that depth of flavor. Be you. If you're happy with the path you are on, then live it up and enjoy it. If you feel your stomach is a jittery mess and your instincts are constantly pushing you to reverse course, take a moment to quiet down all the outside chatter and begin to reconnect with what makes you happy. Practice tuning out all that noise and tuning in to your essence. Seek the roads that permeate you with inspiration—if you can't find them, create one for yourself. When your heart is full, you have joy. When you have joy, you have harmony. And if you have harmony, you can create the life you desire.

One of my greatest joys is hearing people I've known for years say, "Oh, wow, you haven't changed. You're the same silly goof you were back when we met." Yes, and I also have the same feisty mouth I had before my career took off. I just happened to accomplish a few things here and there, but I'm the same person. I'm not good at following instructions, and I enjoy a good challenge—that's why this career is right up my alley. It connects well with who I am. There is a revolutionary in me, a disruptor, a true untamed rebel that is consistently present. And I know this because I know who I am, and I never forgot where I came from.

I value my identity over my success. There is no price for my soul because it's not for sale. A few years back, I used to get offered all kinds of gifts and money from companies hoping to land a contract with us, but I said no every time. Of course, saying yes would've been a violation of Disney's gift and anticorruption policy. But even if that policy didn't exist, my decisions couldn't and cannot be bought. Not by small gifts, not by brand-new BMWs delivered to my front door. I replied politely, "No, I have a car, thanks." I declined it all because I wanted to be able to look at myself in the mirror and say, "Yes, that's still me." I'm the person who put one foot in front of the other to get this far; the one who sometimes puts that same foot in her mouth; and the one who speaks up for what she believes in regardless of the consequences. I never let go of my identity, and all of that translates to the transparency and integrity I bring to my work. That's what you get when you get me.

❮ ❮ ❮

Our sense of identity should always prevail, no matter who we're with or what we do. As my friend Alejo likes to say, "If it makes you happy, that's where you should be." Having said that, we are ever-evolving souls, so what makes us happy today may not make us happy tomorrow. That's the beauty of the power of possibility. Because possibility is change. We tend to reject changing and evolving because we're afraid of what we might find on the other side; we may even fear losing ourselves in the process. But growth is going to come whether we like it or not. Learning from our mistakes, making adjustments, and evolving doesn't mean we have to lose our essence. Knowing who we are actually gives us the confidence we need to take the necessary steps toward a brighter future.

When I was nineteen and I married a man, I didn't know I was going to love a woman in my thirties. When I started my career as a production assistant, I didn't know I would later help run a studio. When I started down my visual effects–producing path in my late twenties, I didn't know it would lead me to working on superhero movies. And I surely didn't know that position would give me the chance to fight for representation on the big and little screen in my forties and fifties. Remaining open to choice and possibility presented those options, and deciding to say yes to those paths while holding on to my essence has led me to where I am today.

❝ ❝ ❝

Marvel's films and series in a way become mirrors for their viewers reflecting not just how they see themselves and connect with the characters but how they may think. In *Ms. Marvel* we featured the first Muslim family and superhero in the MCU, going about their lives in a New Jersey neighborhood with their own everyday struggles and joys. In the scene between Kamala and her BFF Nakia in their high school bathroom, where they are having a heart-to-heart about their search for purpose and identity in the world, Nakia says, "When I first put [my hijab] on, I was hoping to shut some people up, but I kinda realized I don't really need to prove anything to anybody. Like, when I put this on, I feel like me. Like I have a purpose." With a short scene like this one, non-Muslim viewers are invited into a world they might not necessarily know—seeing who these characters are, how they talk to and about each other—therefore raising awareness of issues they may not have understood before. With increased awareness we can learn to respect not just who we are as individuals but who others are too.

At the end of the day, regardless of religion, race, sexual orientation, or where we were born, we are all human beings with hurdles and craters and identity crises. We all want to be loved, we all want to be happy, and we all want to find ourselves. Yet no label will ever encompass all that we are, because we are the sum of all. I am an immigrant, a woman, a lesbian, a mom, a friend, a rebel, and like Carol Danvers says in *Captain Marvel*: "I have nothing to prove to you."

No matter what you do, where you go, who you connect with, always make sure to find your way back to yourself. Focus on doing and being good rather than on your personal gains and achievements. Discover who you are, stay true to yourself no matter how hard the decisions you face may be, live your life with purpose, stay curious, and make sure your identity always prevails.

12

Tap into the Secret Sauce

"Avengers! Assemble."

—CAPTAIN AMERICA, *AVENGERS: ENDGAME* (2019)

Iron Man. That's where it all began. That's where this team first came together: Kevin Feige, now president of Marvel Studios, was the quiet Marvel expert, Louis D'Esposito, now copresident of Marvel Studios, and I were chatty sibling-like freelancers at the time. Three wildly different people united by mutual respect and a zeal to bring Jon Favreau's vision of *Iron Man* to life. As we neared the finish line during postproduction, satisfied with what he had accomplished so far, Kevin offered Louis and me full-time positions at Marvel.

For a moment, I was taken aback. I had never been offered a department head role at a studio before, and it had never been on my radar as one of my career goals. But, not one to shy away from a possibility, I said, "Well, if we were to move forward with this idea, I'd like to have the visual effects and postproduction teams reporting to me so as to have one person at the helm of the movie instead of two people fighting for their individual departments."

Kevin thought about it and replied, "That makes sense. Let's do it."

The three of us continued to enthusiastically talk about the opportunity before us, what we would do differently, and what we would improve based on what we had observed on other jobs. The power of possibility was tingling at our fingertips. We wanted to change the game and perhaps one day become the studio and creative force that did it all. So we agreed to team up, assemble, take that leap together, and do it right.

In 2008, after striking a deal with Manhattan Beach Studios, we moved out of the office above the car dealership in Beverly Hills and went on to film *Iron Man 2* and several other movies at this facility, which became our base for subsequent years as we set our plan in motion. We wanted our studio to be reminiscent of the old Hollywood studios that had every department under one big umbrella. In our case, it started with having a shared special effects department, stunt department, and prop master, to name a few. The goal: to attempt to make more than one movie at a time and use the same teams on different productions. By doing so, if one project hit a snag, the teams could focus on the other productions, and we could potentially avoid losing money and time while waiting for the issue to be resolved. As we continued to grow, we kept this model in place in Los Angeles, and later replicated it in

London, Atlanta, and other locations. Then, when we added the stereo and technology department, I volunteered to take it over because it's all linked to VFX and postproduction, and Kevin and Lou agreed. It was now a reality: the teams, the vision, the studio.

In the following eighteen years that Kevin, Lou, and I worked together to bring more than thirty Marvel films and shows to the big and small screens, we've been asked time and again, "How did you do it? What's the secret?" I never knew quite how to answer this question. We didn't devise a surefire magic formula in a lab that would guarantee success. What is the elusive secret sauce that made Marvel Studios such a ginormous success? A heaping spoonful of the strength that we found in our differences, a hearty helping of mutual respect, all finished with the magic of collaboration.

❝ ❝ ❝

Before Kamala Harris became the US vice president, I met her at a luncheon she attended for Latinas, and she said one phrase that day that stuck with me: "In our differences lie our strengths." I later realized she was likely paraphrasing renowned American educator Stephen Covey, who once wrote, "Strength lies in differences, not in similarities." Interestingly, from my experience, very few people see this as a plus, especially nowadays when we seem to be more divided than ever as a society. In truth, at first glance, it may not be the most practical or intuitive secret sauce ingredient. Differences mean that it may take us longer to reach a conclusion, an answer, a final cut. Differences require patience. But the longer journey allows us to look at what we are making from different viewpoints, ideas, and sentiments. This not only enriches the path we are on but also delivers a more carefully thought-out and well-shaped result than the one we would have reached had we all been standing in the same corner observing our project through the same lens from the same perspective.

Kevin, Lou, and I were no exception. There were our different personalities: Kevin was quiet and reserved, highly focused on all things superheroes, the stories, the characters, the timelines. Meanwhile, although Lou and I might have had differing points of view and backgrounds, we were both personable and loved to talk, talk, talk about everything and anything. I actually loved and appreciated many of our agile political conversations. When in a room discussing a project, Kevin was the one who could remember lines from different versions of a script or scene, even if they were only changed by three words. He'd casually say something like "Well, on version twenty-seven, we have this moment, and I think that line made a difference." And I'd just stare back at him in awe and say, "How do you remember that?" I always used to tell him I believed he had an elephant's memory. Lou has that gift too. I have that recall power with imagery but not with scripts.

My path has always been visual storytelling, whether it was in the form of a thirty-second commercial, a two-hour play, or a TV show or film. It's no coincidence that most of the musicians I'm attracted to are storytellers too, like Joan Manuel Serrat and Silvio Rodríguez, the old troubadours who don't just sing but narrate an adventure or life experience with their songs. Now, if you sit me down to read . . . Well, I'm a terrible reader. As a young girl, I could never focus my concentration long enough to get through a book. Black-and-white pages with words make my mind wander. It can take me two to three hours to read a regular 120-page script, which my colleagues can flip through in fifty minutes. I start off fine, but by page two, I hold on to a concept and my mind begins to meander into different possibilities of how we could bring it to life, and I become lost in my own little world. With time, I've developed techniques to lock myself on the ever-elusive page.

First, I need a quiet space with as few distractions as possible. If my dogs are rowdy or there's something going on outside my window, I will be up and out of there in a heartbeat and won't return for a long while. Once I'm focused, I like to doodle in the margins. That keeps my attention on the page and away from any surrounding activity. My go-to is drawing small three-dimensional cubes because they represent every point of view—mine, yours, and theirs—and they're always connected. I also like to create a waterfall effect or some other shape with movement.

Processing information visually is one of my strengths. Much like Kevin and Lou with scripts, I can look at three slightly different versions of an image and quickly identify if you changed two trees on the hill. So yes, it may take me a while to get through a script, but give me an image to work with and I can spend hours dissecting the story it holds. No matter how repetitive the process may seem, I always find something new in the moving image.

These differences balanced us out and allowed us to have every corner covered as a team at Marvel. Our strengths came through at different times during the development, preproduction, production, postproduction, and marketing of our films, and we learned to lean on one another as we danced our way through the process. For example, while Kevin homed in on the devoted fans, I always said, "Give it to me as if I've never seen anything Marvel-related." This balance kept the existing fans happy, with Easter eggs for those in the know, while also making the projects accessible to new viewers, which in turn created longevity for the franchise.

In our differences lay the beauty of our experience. Our three points of view and different roles made our stories tighter, and we consistently upheld our mutual respect. We are quirky people, but we learned to like and respect one another's quirks. That allowed us to listen beyond our differences and leave the door open for new and unexpected ideas that helped make the stories better, whether creatively or technically.

Throughout the years, the three of us maintained an unspoken agreement: The franchise was the most important ego to feed. We always supported the best story, idea, or process, no matter who came up with it. And it didn't end with us. We built a diverse team of people at Marvel, some who were there with us from the start and others who joined us along the way, but everyone played an important role in creating the more than thirty films and shows we made together. The combination of all our talents made us a stronger whole.

❮ ❮ ❮

The final star ingredient in our secret sauce was our power of collaboration. From day one, we shared a single trailer on set, where we talked through the issues with the creative producer assigned to each project and came up with the solutions. We'd eat lunch together and were practically inseparable. It was part of what made us so efficient. The more we were together, the more we could solve and get done. During one of these stints of living and breathing one of our projects, I blurted out, "Okay, I may be going to the island with this, but . . ." It was like a reverse *Survivor* reference. Instead of being voted off the island, what I had to say might get me voted off the mainland. In other words, I basically had an out-of-the-box idea that I knew might be rejected at first, but I had to throw it out there anyway, even if it meant having to paddle to the island afterward. "Going to the island" eventually became part of our lexicon. We all went to the island and that was okay, even welcomed.

Rejected ideas are never something to be ashamed of, because they're not personal. Our disagreements were solely based on the characters and the stories, not on our personal opinions. The resounding question throughout the years, throughout the long list of writers, producers, and directors, was always "What would the character do?" The characters, the stories, the franchise, that's what we were consistently out to protect. This allowed us to foster a creative and safe space where everyone in the room felt comfortable expressing themselves without judgment, no matter how far-fetched the thought might have seemed at the time. What's more, even if our ideas landed us on the island at first, their essence lingered and sometimes sparked another solution that would fill the gap we had been staring at. So say your idea, no matter how off the charts it may sound, and if needed, go to the island—and come back with another idea to see if that one sticks.

I remember one time, while working on *Avengers: Infinity War*, we kept coming back to a specific scene, wondering how to best handle it. It was in the middle of the epic battle sequence, when the Scarlet Witch is sideswiped by Proxima Midnight, who stands over the Scarlet Witch and says, "He'll die alone," referring to Vision, "as will you." And Black Widow comes up from behind and replies, "She's not alone." Proxima turns to find Black Widow in a fighting stance on one side and Okoye with her spear on the other. The scene was problematic because in the test screening we received feedback that it interrupted the flow of the epic battle on-screen. Still, Marvel fought to keep it in the film as we knew it was important for women. Silence was not an option. The message delivered in that line was far greater than imagined because it was telling women that we are not alone as women. This wasn't about girl power. This was about seeing strong women stand up for themselves and fight for one another. This was empowerment. And this line eventually became one of the most memorable Black Widow quotes across the globe.

During the eighteen years I worked at Marvel, we focused on creating better stories, working together to figure out how we could make a shot more dynamic, how we could make the light shine brighter and better, and how we could improve the dialogue, and it was a thrilling experience. Teamwork at its finest. I felt I had found a place where my voice was heard, where I could be myself, and where I could freely express "go to the island" ideas, take the leap, and not be shut out, because we fostered the embracing of our differences. We spent close to two decades building that behemoth of a studio together, leaning on one another, remaining in the trenches side by side through thick and thin, telling stories that I'm proud to say have become part of our legacy. And as with all great stories, this one too was approaching its end.

13

Part of Every Journey Is the End

"Part of the journey is the end."

—IRON MAN, *AVENGERS: ENDGAME* (2019)

Every journey we embark on, be it a short stroll or an epic adventure, has a beginning, a middle, and an end. Each step we take is a choice that will come with consequences. They will either push us forward, to the side, or backward. The key is to continuously be aware of our actions, consciously making decisions that will later prevent us from succumbing to living in regret. We also have to be okay with reaching our destination. Because that's what the end is, a destination, the place we arrive at before launching into new beginnings filled with more possibilities. In my own journey, I have always chosen to keep moving forward, even if that means I may eventually have to cross the threshold and exit the building after reaching my destination.

Having to leave behind something that you helped create can be excruciatingly difficult, but sometimes a life's purpose goes far beyond what we ever imagined. Take Iron Man, for example. As difficult and heartrending as it was to say goodbye to Tony Stark in *Avengers: Endgame,* we had the chance to see the beautiful arc of his story unfold over the years, from cocky know-it-all to a man who became a superhero, saved those in need, suffered panic attacks, learned to love and be loved, started a family, and ultimately sacrificed his own life for the greater good. Letting him go was a daunting decision, but it gifted us with the opportunity to portray what is possible when someone is not willing to compromise their beliefs, identity, or integrity.

One of the things I love about the Marvel movies I worked on through the years is that they are filled with layers. Sure, on the surface, there's the classic conflict-resolution superhero story, but if you take time to peel back that top layer, embedded in certain scenes are underlying questions waiting to be discovered: *Are we our jobs? Is our identity linked to that one thing we do? Who do we choose to become?* As the studio grew exponentially year after year, it began to affect the way we worked. Occasionally it felt like our time and energy were diminished. Kevin, Lou, and I had so much on our plates, between the demands of a job that always needed us and personal lives that also deserved attention, that even being in the same room for a long period became a feat at times. Finding balance was elusive, but we powered through, doing the best that we could because that was good enough.

I'm still a work in progress on the balance note, but I believe having my child opened a door I hadn't explored before. Children give us permission to stop. Wouldn't it be great if we were able to do that for ourselves too? Instead of saying "I have to leave early to get to my kid's parent-teacher conference," wouldn't it be great if we felt we could say "I have to leave early because I have a conference with myself I can't miss"? But we don't have the license to say that at work. Society is not there yet, but we should strive to reach that turning point one day. Our time for ourselves should be just as important as the time we take off to care for others. Getting a massage, going on a hike, reading a book, playing tennis—those moments that bring us joy and peace help recharge our batteries, and, in turn, our work reaps the benefits of a calmer and more well-rested mind.

In the process of exploring the myriad questions that are planted in our movies, I found myself wondering about similar questions. *Am I doing what I love? What would I do if I didn't have this job? Would my ego allow me to reinvent myself, or would it throw me into a state of depression, like Dr. Strange after his accident?* And, despite the ever-increasing demands, the answers were always resounding: Yes, I was doing what I loved. And yes, if I lost it all, I knew I would find a way to reinvent myself. When you are hurled into the open sea unexpectedly, it won't always be sunny. There will be days with no wind when you feel you may be floating aimlessly with no land in sight. Storms will roll in and wreak havoc on your raft. And you may not end up on the shore you had envisioned. But that will be the shore you needed to reach.

€ € €

When I first joined Marvel, I didn't like superheroes and I had never helped run a studio, but I tapped into my power of possibility and thought, *Well, why not?* Then I went higher, further, and faster, but I never lost sight of who I am. I continued to use my voice to speak up, to push boundaries, and in the process, my nonnegotiables began to once again shift and my purpose became clearer. Now it was no longer just about staying local; it was about wielding my power to help marginalized communities be seen and heard, not as outcasts but as part of the everyday fabric of our society. And I chose to do so using the podium of art rather than politics because this medium allows me to reach far beyond a political base. Films allow me to attempt to show people from all walks of life that there is far more that unites us than divides us. Movies are a conduit for hope and possibility.

€ € €

I do believe everything happens for you, not to you. What's more, part of our greatest moments of reinvention come from the second chances we are handed—that "take two" in life, love, work. These moments may be difficult to get through, to understand, to process, but if we do it with grace—without opting to sit in the victim's chair, and by choosing love over hate or anger or resentment—then we will be all the stronger for it. Our lows are like big-wave surfing in Nazaré, Portugal, and suddenly being wiped out. We must swim back to the beach, dig the seaweed from our hair, shake out the pesky pockets of sand in our suits, and catch our breath, to finally see that every step we have taken has been leading us here, to the shore of a new beginning. If I had to do it over, I wouldn't do anything differently. I'm at peace with my choices. I stand by them. Knowledge and truth are my shield and armor; they may not protect me from pain, but they guard me against regret.

As we pull ourselves out of the craters in our lives and dust ourselves off, let's take a moment to carefully observe our surroundings. Because amid the debris of what once was, there are seedlings of new possibilities. Even in the darkest of times, the power of possibility's pulse does not wane. It is there, steady, beating along our side as we end certain journeys and pave the way to new ones. For many people, a career may be a lifetime of the same choice. For others, it's about the possibilities beyond that one path. Especially when you hit your fifties. By now we have proven what we are capable of, we have proven our worth, and all that's left is to make sure we are happy. When you no longer feel nourished by what you do, when your curiosity is no longer fed, when you start feeling like you fit in but you don't truly belong, then take a beat to reevaluate your journey and consider a new path.

Start by asking yourself this: *Do I want to fit in, or do I want to belong?* Fitting in means assimilating to your surroundings, changing yourself to match your environment in order to be accepted. Belonging is a place where you can be who you are and never feel that you're not welcome. I remember hearing Julie Ann Crommett—diversity and inclusion master, and founder and CEO of Collective Moxie—share this concept on belonging: "The difference between fitting in and belonging is that when you fit in, they ask you to the dance, but when you belong, they play your music." That stuck with me. I look back at my life and often wonder how a girl from La Plata, Argentina, got to become a top executive at a film studio with the highest-grossing film franchise of all time. It didn't seem plausible on the surface. But I believed in something better. I knew telling stories would be my way of expanding my horizons. And I always strived and continue to strive to be in a room where they play my music and allow me to shine for who I am in my entirety.

Life may get the best of us at times, but the journey of our spirit has no boundaries or limitations. If we remain open and aware of our steps and our choices, we will be able to see rivulets of light breaching the depths of our craters, gifting us with glimmers of hope. There are many stories I have in my heart that I still hope to help tell one day. There are many more dreams I want to turn into reality. When all is said and done, endings are not the culmination of our dreams—they are just doors to new beginnings filled with endless possibilities.

No matter where you are along your path, no matter what

you have experienced and survived, you continue to be all potential, you continue to have the freedom to choose your best way forward and live in the light rather than the darkness, and you continue to have your voice to speak out. Believe in yourself. The power of possibility lives within you.

"Heroes are made by the path they choose,
not the powers they are graced with."

—IRON MAN, *IRON MAN* (2008)

Acknowledgments

These pages have seen me through breathtaking peaks and crater-filled valleys, through cherished moments of pure joy and some of the stormiest times of my life. Nothing is permanent except the lessons we learn along the way and the possibility of a better tomorrow. As I constantly chose to live in the light regardless of the circumstances, I also had an invaluable circle of friends, family, and colleagues who stood by my side through the incessant twists and turns along my path. Thank you, gracias de todo corazón. . . .

To Raven, my beautiful, loving child, for turning storms into sunshine. Your magnificent being encourages me to persevere through whatever life throws at me so that I can help build a future full of promise for you. I love you.

To Imelda, for two decades of love and light and for teaching me endless lessons.

To Alejo, my best friend and chosen brother, for knowing my

core, loving all of me, and making me laugh a carcajadas through it all. I can't picture a life without you in it.

To Elena, for being the best chosen sister life can gift you, for the many conversations about the infinite possibilities that were only on the other side of madness.

To Luz María Doria, for opening my eyes to the possibility of writing a book and for pushing me relentlessly to take that leap, no matter how hesitant I seemed. Thank you for believing in me, and for your unwavering friendship.

To Johanna Castillo, my fierce and passionate literary agent; from the moment Luz María introduced us, I felt you got me. Thank you for guiding me through the book publishing process and standing by my side while I rode one of the most challenging roller coasters of my life.

To Cecilia Molinari, my writing partner and friend, for sorting through all my meandering thoughts and helping me turn them into my story on these pages, for the constant insight into all the hurdles that this process has thrown at us, and for always reminding me that words can change someone's day. Thank you for the never-ending joy you brought to this unknown journey and, more importantly, for trusting me to do something you do so well. This book would not have been finished without you. I am forever grateful you were my writing partner! Gracias, amiga querida.

To Adam Wilson, executive editor at Hyperion Avenue, for your patience, kindness, thoughtful edits and suggestions, and guidance through every stage of this bookmaking process. I'm grateful this project landed in your hands. And thank you to editor Chelsea Cutchens for your careful line edits, and the entire Hyperion Avenue team for bringing this book to life.

And to you, dear reader, holding this book in your hands, thank you for taking the time to pore over my thoughts and experiences. If anything, I hope my story inspires you to pursue your dreams and consider the endless possibilities that await you on the other side of the doors on your path. Ultimately, you are the superhero in your life. Never forget that.